AAT

Level 4

Diploma in Professional Accounting

Personal Tax FA 2025

Exam Practice Kit

For assessments from 26th January 2026 to 24th January 2027

BPP

Ninth edition 2025

ISBN 9781 0355 3047 2

Previous ISBN 9781 0355 1654 4

eISBN 9781 0355 3065 6

British Library Cataloguing-in-Publication Data

A catalogue record for this book is available from the British Library

Published by

BPP Learning Media Ltd
BPP House, Aldine Place
142–144 Uxbridge Road
London W12 8AA

learningmedia.bpp.com

Your learning materials are printed on paper obtained from traceable sustainable sources.

All rights reserved. No part of this publication may be reproduced, stored in a retrieval system or transmitted in any form or by any means, graphic, electronic or mechanical including photocopying, recording or otherwise, without the prior written permission of the publisher.

The contents of these learning materials are intended as a guide and not professional advice. Although every effort has been made to ensure that the contents of this book are correct at the time of going to press, BPP makes no warranty that the information in this book is accurate or complete and accept no liability for any loss or damage suffered by any person acting or refraining from acting as a result of the material in these learning materials.

© BPP Learning Media Ltd 2025

A note about copyright

Breach of copyright is a form of theft. Without the express permission of BPP you are breaching copyright if you:

- Photocopy our materials
- Print our digital materials in order to share them with or forward them to a third party or use them in any way other than in connection with your BPP studies
- Distribute our digital materials online (including sharing them with third parties and uploading them to websites)

Please note that eBooks are sold on a single user licence basis.

NO AI TRAINING. Unless otherwise agreed in writing, the use of BPP material for the purpose of AI training is not permitted. Any use of this material to "train" generative artificial intelligence (AI) technologies is prohibited, as is providing archived or cached data sets containing such material to another person or entity.

Contents

Introduction

This is BPP Learning Media's AAT Exam Practice Kit for *Personal Tax*. It is part of a suite of ground-breaking resources produced by BPP Learning Media for AAT assessments.

This Exam Practice Kit has been written in conjunction with the BPP Course Book, and has been carefully designed to enable students to practise all of the learning outcomes and assessment criteria for the units that make up Personal Tax. It is fully up to date as at August 2025 and reflects both the AAT's qualification specification and the practice assessment provided by the AAT.

This Exam Practice Kit contains tasks corresponding to each chapter of the Course Book. Some tasks are designed for learning purposes, others are of assessment standard.

The emphasis in all tasks and assessments is on the practical application of the skills acquired.

Assessments from 26 January 2026 will use the rules contained in Finance Act 2025 and tasks will focus on tax rates and thresholds for the tax year 2025/26.

It may be that you have to deal with other tax years at work, in which case the rates and thresholds you use will be different.

This Exam Practice Kit is focused on your assessment from 26 January 2026. At the time of writing, no end date has been provided by AAT. You should check their website for the validity of this Exam Practice Kit for assessments from 2027.

Approaching the assessment

When you sit the assessment it is very important that you follow the on screen instructions. This means you need to carefully read the instructions, both on the introduction screens and during specific tasks.

When you access the assessment you should be presented with an introductory screen with information similar to that shown below (taken from the introductory screen from the AAT's Q2022 Practice Assessment for *Personal Tax*).

Assessment information:

You have **2 1/2 hours** to complete this sample assessment.

- This assessment contains **10 tasks** and you should attempt to complete every task.
- Each task is independent. You will not need to refer to your answers in previous tasks.
- The total number of marks for this assessment is 100.
- Read every task carefully to make sure you understand what is required.
- Where the date is relevant, it is given in the task data.
- Both minus signs or brackets can be used to indicate negative numbers **unless** task instructions say otherwise.
- You must use a full stop to indicate a decimal point. For example, write 100.57 NOT 100,57 or 100 57.
- You may use a comma to indicate a number in the thousands, but you don't have to. For example, 10000 and 10,000 are both acceptable.
- If your answer requires rounding, apply normal mathematical rules **unless** the task instructions say otherwise.

The actual instructions will vary depending on the subject you are studying for. It is very important you read the instructions on the introductory screen and apply them in the assessment. You don't want to lose marks when you know the correct answer just because you have not entered it in the right format.

In general, the rules set out in the AAT practice assessments for the subject you are studying for will apply in the real assessment, but you should carefully read the information on this screen again in the real assessment, just to make sure.

A full stop is needed to indicate a decimal point. We would recommend using minus signs to indicate negative numbers and leaving out the comma signs to indicate thousands, as this results in a lower number of keystrokes and less margin for error when working under time pressure. Having said that, you can use whatever is easiest for you as long as you operate within the rules set out for your particular assessment.

You have to show competence throughout the assessment, and you should therefore complete all of the tasks. Don't leave questions unanswered.

Written or complex tasks will be human marked. In this case you are given a blank space or table to enter your answer into. You are told in the assessments which tasks these are.

When these involve calculations, it is a good idea to decide in advance how you are going to lay out your answers to such tasks by practising answering them on a word document, and certainly you should try all such tasks in this Exam Practice Kit and in the AAT's environment using the sample assessment.

When asked to fill in tables, or gaps, never leave any blank even if you are unsure of the answer. Fill in your best estimate.

Note that for some assessments where there is a lot of scenario information or tables of data provided (eg tax tables), you may need to access these via 'pop-ups'. Instructions will be provided on how you can bring up the necessary data during the assessment.

Finally, take note of any task specific instructions once you are in the assessment. For example, you may be asked to enter a date in a certain format or to enter a number to a certain number of decimal places.

Grading

To achieve the qualification and to be awarded a grade, you must pass all the mandatory unit assessments, all optional unit assessments (where applicable) and the synoptic assessment.

The AAT Level 4 Professional Diploma in Accounting will be awarded a grade. This grade will be based on performance across the qualification. Unit assessments and synoptic assessments are not individually graded. These assessments are given a mark that is used in calculating the overall grade.

How overall grade is determined

You will be awarded an overall qualification grade (Distinction, Merit, and Pass). If you do not achieve the qualification you will not receive a qualification certificate, and the grade will be shown as unclassified.

The marks of each assessment will be converted into a percentage mark and rounded up or down to the nearest whole number. This percentage mark is then weighted according to the weighting of the unit assessment or synoptic assessment within the qualification. The resulting weighted assessment percentages are combined to arrive at a percentage mark for the whole qualification.

Grade definition	Percentage threshold
Distinction	90–100%
Merit	80–89%
Pass	70–79%
Unclassified	0–69% Or failure to pass one or more assessments

Resits

The AAT Professional Diploma In Accounting is not subject to re-sit restrictions.

You should only be entered for an assessment when you are well-prepared and you expect to pass the assessment.

AAT qualifications

The material in this book may support the following AAT qualifications:

AAT Professional Diploma in Accounting Level 4, AAT Professional Diploma in Accounting at SCQF Level 8.

Supplements

From time to time we may need to publish supplementary materials to one of our titles. This can be for a variety of reasons. From a small change in the AAT unit guidance to new legislation coming into effect between editions.

You should check our supplements page regularly for anything that may affect your learning materials. All supplements are available free of charge on our supplements page on our website at:

learningmedia.bpp.com

Improving material and removing errors

BPP Learning Media do everything possible to ensure the material is accurate and up to date when sending to print. In the event that any errors are found after the print date, they are uploaded to the following website: learningmedia.bpp.com/pages/errata.

AAT Practice Assessment

The AAT practice assessments mimic the real exam and so must be attempted prior to taking the real exam. You should attempt these using a laptop/desktop computer, as this will give you a better feel for the actual AAT exam conditions.

Please note, at the end of each test you will be presented with feedback which you should review.

Use this link below to access the assessment required: https://www.aat.org.uk/learning-portal.

Questions

Chapter 1 – Taxable income

Task 1.1

For each of the following sources of income, indicate whether it is non-savings income, savings income or dividend income by ticking the relevant box:

	Non-savings income ✓	Savings income ✓	Dividend income ✓
Trading income			
Dividend received from a company			
Property income			
Building society interest			
Bank interest			
Pension income			
Employment income			
Interest from government stock ('gilts')			

Task 1.2

Olive received the following income in 2025/26.

Required

Show the amount of income that she should enter on her tax return. If the income is exempt, enter 0.

(a) Bank account interest £160

£ [ ]

(b) Premium bond prize £100

£ [ ]

(c) Dividends £540

£ [ ]

Task 1.3

For each of the following income sources, indicate whether they are received gross, net of tax or are exempt from income tax by ticking the relevant box:

	Gross ✓	Net ✓	Exempt ✓
Bank interest			
Interest on an individual savings account (ISA)			
Employment income			

	Gross ✓	Net ✓	Exempt ✓
Interest from government stock ('gilts')			

Task 1.4

You act for Jonty. The following information is relevant for the year ended 5 April 2026:

(1) His salary was £38,800.

(2) His other income received was:

	£
Building society interest	80
Dividends	63

Required

Jonty's taxable income for 2025/26 is:

£ [ ]

Task 1.5

Mr Betteredge has the following income for 2025/26:

	£
Salary for the year to 5 April 2026	15,665
Interest received (amount received shown):	
National Westminster Bank plc	457
ISA account	180
Nationwide Building Society account	400

Required

Using the proforma layout provided, prepare a schedule of income for 2025/26, clearly showing the distinction between non-savings and savings income. If income is exempt, enter 0. Mr Betteredge's personal allowance should be deducted as appropriate. Fill in ALL the unshaded boxes and add a 0 (zero) if necessary.

	Non-savings income £	Savings income £	Total £
Earnings			
Bank deposit interest			
Building society interest			
ISA interest			
Net income			
Less personal allowance			

	Non-savings income £	Savings income £	Total £
Taxable income			

QUESTIONS

Task 1.6

Hayley receives employment income of £95,000, bank interest of £1,600, ISA interest of £2,000 and dividends of £4,500 in 2025/26.

Required

(a) Hayley's net income for 2025/26 is:

£ [ ]

(b) The personal allowance that Hayley is entitled to for 2025/26 is:

£ [ ]

Task 1.7

Max has net income of £116,000 for 2025/26. He made Gift Aid donations of £4,000 (gross) during the year.

Required

Max's personal allowance for 2025/26 is:

£ [ ]

Task 1.8

In 2025/26, Gavin receives pension income of £19,300, bank interest of £2,000, dividends of £5,400 and lottery winnings of £6,000.

Required

(a) Gavin's net income for 2025/26 is:

£ [ ]

(b) The personal allowance that Gavin is entitled to for 2025/26 is:

£ [ ]

Task 1.9

For the tax year 2025/26 the maximum an individual can invest for the tax year in an ISA is:

£ [ ]

Task 1.10

Tick to show whether the following statement is True or False.

Scholarships and educational grants are exempt as income of the student.

	✓
True	
False	

Task 1.11

Tick to show whether the following statement is True or False.

Damages received for an injury at work are only sometimes exempt from income tax, whereas damages paid on death are always exempt from income tax.

	✓
True	
False	

Chapter 2 – Calculation of income tax

Task 2.1

Guy receives bank interest of £7,500 in 2025/26.

Required

Calculate the income tax liability assuming he has non savings income before PA of:

(a) **£12,850 (show whole pounds only)**

£ [ ]

(b) **£51,850 (show whole pounds only)**

£ [ ]

Task 2.2

You act for Deidre Watkins. Deidre has the following taxable income for 2025/26:

Non-savings income	£14,700
Savings income	£2,176
Dividend income	£1,266

Required

Calculate Deidre's tax liability (show whole pounds only) on each source of income for 2025/26 as follows:

(a) **Non-savings income:**

£ [ ]

(b) **Savings income:**

£ [ ]

(c) **Dividend income:**

£ [ ]

Task 2.3

Peter has non-savings income of £205,000 and makes a personal pension contribution of £12,000 in December 2025.

Required

Tick to show the amount of Peter's additional rate threshold in 2025/26.

	✓
£125,140	
£137,140	
£140,140	
£128,140	

Task 2.4

Tony is a higher rate taxpayer and makes a Gift Aid donation of £6,000 in December 2025.

Required

Tick to show the amount of Tony's basic rate band in 2025/26.

	✓
£43,700	
£37,700	
£45,200	
£30,200	

Task 2.5

Katy is an additional rate taxpayer and makes a Gift Aid donation of £4,000 in June 2025.

Required

(a) Katy's basic rate band for 2025/26 is:

£ [ ]

(b) Katy's additional rate threshold for 2025/26 is:

£ [ ]

(c) Katy's higher rate band for 2025/26 is:

£ [ ]

Task 2.6

Ruth has non-savings income of £30,000, savings income of £2,000 and dividend income of £6,000.

Required

(a) Ruth's personal savings allowance for 2025/26 is:

£ [ ]

(b) Ruth's dividend allowance for 2025/26 is:

£ [ ]

Task 2.7

Rachel received £24,420 bank interest in 2025/26. This is her only income.

Required

Rachel's income tax payable for 2025/26 is:

£ [ ]

Task 2.8

Richard has taxable non-savings income of £58,525 in 2025/26. He made pension contributions to his personal pension scheme of £10,800 during the year. Tax of £9,700 was deducted under the PAYE system.

Required

Richard's income tax payable for 2025/26 is:

£ [ ]

Task 2.9

John Smith has the following income and outgoings for the tax year 2025/26:

	£
Salary (£7,570 tax deducted under PAYE)	50,850
Interest on a deposit account with the Scotia Bank	800
Donation under the Gift Aid scheme made on 1 September 2025	2,400
Dividends received on UK shares	500

Required

(a) Using the proforma layout provided, prepare a schedule of income for 2025/26, clearly showing the distinction between non-savings, savings and dividend income. Fill in all the unshaded boxes. If an answer is zero input 0.

	Non-savings income £	Savings income £	Dividend income £	Total £
Salary				
Dividend				
Bank deposit interest				
Net income				
Less personal allowance				
Taxable income				

(b) John's income tax liability for 2025/26 is:

£ [ ]

(c) John's income tax payable for 2025/26 is:

£ [ ]

Task 2.10

Jean Brown has the following income and outgoings for the tax year 2025/26:

	£
Salary (£48,500 tax deducted under PAYE)	155,000

	£
Interest on a bank deposit account	3,000
Personal pension contribution	8,000
Dividends received on UK shares	10,000

Required

(a) Using the proforma layout provided, prepare a schedule of income for 2025/26, clearly showing the distinction between non-savings, savings and dividend income. Fill in all the unshaded boxes. If an answer is zero input 0.

	Non-savings income £	Savings income £	Dividend income £	Total £
Salary				
Dividend				
Bank deposit interest				
Net income				
Less personal allowance				
Taxable income				

(b) Jean's income tax liability for 2025/26 is:

£ [ ]

(c) Jean's income tax payable for 2025/26 is:

£ [ ]

Task 2.11

This style of task is human marked in the live assessment.

During 2025/26 Joshua has income as follows:

Pension income £10,050

Bank interest received £11,145

Dividends received £9,500

Joshua made a Gift Aid donation of £1,500 in July 2025.

Required

Calculate Joshua's total income tax liability for 2025/26, using the table given below. Show your answer in whole pounds.

	£	£	£	£

	£	£	£	£

Task 2.12

This style of task is human marked in the live assessment.

During 2025/26 Jack has income as follows:

Trading income	£90,000
Bank interest received	£1,500
Dividends received	£15,000

Required

Calculate Jack's total income tax liability for 2025/26, using the table given below. Show your answer in whole pounds.

	£	£	£	£

	£	£	£	£

Chapter 3 – Employment income

Task 3.1

Show whether the following statement is True or False.

An employee has a contract for services.

	✓
True	
False	

Task 3.2

Peter undertakes some work for XYZ plc.

Required

Tick which of the following factors would indicate that he either has a contract of service with XYZ plc or a contract for services.

Factor	Contract of service ✓	Contract for services ✓
Peter is entitled to paid holidays		
Peter hires his own helpers		
Peter takes substantial financial risks when undertaking work for XYZ plc		
Peter does not have to rectify mistakes in his work at his own expense		

Task 3.3

Emma is employed as a retail salesperson and provides you with the following information about what she has received from her employer:

(1) Monthly salary of £2,000 paid on the first of each month until September 2025, with a 2% increase starting from 1 October 2025

(2) Commission of £1,000 earned during a special sales event in March 2026, paid with the May 2026 salary

(3) Employer's contribution of 5% of salary on 31 March 2026 to company's occupational pension scheme

(4) Bonus of £1,200 received 30 April 2025, based on company's accounting profit for the year ended 31 March 2025

Required

For each item, show the amount that will be taxable in 2025/26:

Use whole numbers, and if the answer is zero, write 0.

Item	£
Salary	
Commission	
Employer's pension contribution	
Bonus	

Task 3.4

Show whether the following statement is true or false.

Tips received by a tour guide from customers are not earnings.

	✓
True	
False	

Task 3.5

A director of a company is entitled to a bonus for her employer's year ended 31 December 2025. The bonus is determined on 30 November 2025, credited to her director's account on 20 December 2025 and is actually paid to her on 6 January 2026.

Required

The date of receipt of the bonus for employment income purposes is: (insert date as XX/XX/XXXX)

[ ]

Task 3.6

Mo was provided with a petrol engine car by her employer on 6 August 2025. The car cost the employer £13,500 and the list price of the car was £15,000. The car's CO_2 emissions were 142 g/km.

Required

(a) The cost of the car in the taxable benefit computation is:

£ [ ]

(b) The percentage used in the taxable benefit computation is:

[ ] %

(c) The taxable benefit on the provision of the car is:

£ [ ]

Task 3.7

Frank was provided with a new car with a list price of £25,000 on 6 June 2025. The firm paid for all fuel (£2,300) without requiring any payment by Frank for fuel for private use. However, he was required to pay the firm £35 per month for the private use of the car itself. The car has CO_2 emissions of 138 g/km.

Required

(a) The taxable benefit on the provision of the car is:

£ ☐

(b) The taxable benefit on the provision of fuel is:

£ ☐

Task 3.8

Julian is provided with a company car for business and private use throughout 2025/26. The car had a list price of £11,500 when purchased, although the company paid £10,000 for the car after a dealer discount. It has CO_2 emissions of 72 g/km. The company pays for all running costs, including all fuel. Julian does not make any contribution for his private use of the car.

Required

(a) The cost of the car in the taxable benefit computation is:

£ ☐

(b) The percentage used in the taxable benefit computation is:

☐ %

(c) The taxable benefit in respect of the provision of fuel for private use is:

£ ☐

Task 3.9

Sarah works for XXM plc and is provided with a company car for business and private use throughout 2025/26.

The car has CO_2 emissions of 194 g/km. It has a list price of £57,000. Sarah agreed to make a capital contribution of £6,000 towards the cost of the car. The company pays for all running costs, including all fuel. Sarah pays £50 a month towards the cost of private fuel – the actual cost of private fuel is about £90 a month.

Required

(a) Tick to show which percentage is used in the taxable benefit computation.

	✓
27	
37	
17	
44	

(b) **The taxable benefit in respect of the provision of the car is:**

£ [ ]

(c) **The taxable benefit in respect of the provision of the fuel for private use is:**

£ [ ]

Task 3.10

Francine is employed by Bale plc as a delivery driver and is supplied with a van, which she parks overnight at home. She uses the van to drive to the company's depot to pick up packages but otherwise is not allowed to use the van for her own private purposes. The company provides fuel for the van. The cost of fuel for driving the van from her home to the depot is £500 for 2025/26.

Required

Tick to show the taxable benefit for Francine in respect of the van for 2025/26.

	✓
£4,020	
£4,789	
£769	
Nil	

Task 3.11

A camera costing £200 is bought by an employer for the private use of an employee on 6 April 2024. The camera is purchased by the employee for £50 on 6 April 2025, when its market value is £120.

Required

The taxable benefit for 2025/26 is:

£ [ ]

Task 3.12

On 6 April 2025 an employer made a loan of £50,000 to an employee. The employee repaid £20,000 on 6 December 2025. The remaining £30,000 was outstanding at 5 April 2026. Interest paid during the year was £725. The official rate of interest was 3.75% throughout 2025/26.

Required

(a) **Using the average method, the taxable benefit for 2025/26 is:**

£ [ ]

(b) **Using the alternative method, the taxable benefit for 2025/26 is:**

£ [ ]

Task 3.13

Tick to show whether the following statement is true or false.

If a loan of £7,000 to an employee is written-off and this is the only loan to the employee by the employer, there is no taxable benefit.

	✓
True	
False	

Task 3.14

Vimal is given the use of a new television, costing £1,000, by his employer on 1 January 2024. Vimal subsequently buys the television from his employer for £100 on 1 January 2026 when it is worth £300.

Required

(a) The taxable benefit for 2025/26 is:

£ [ ]

The television is used to keep Vimal entertained when living at 3 Sims Court, London EC1, a flat provided by his employer. The flat cost £131,250 five years ago when Vimal moved in, but due to a slump in property prices is now only worth £90,000. It has an annual value of £3,000. The official rate of interest is 3.75%.

Required

(b) The taxable benefit for 2025/26 is:

£ [ ]

Task 3.15

Giles receives a salary of £25,000 and has received the following benefits from his employer throughout 2025/26:

(1) Free medical insurance – the cost to the company is £385 per annum, although if Giles had taken this out privately, he would have to pay £525.

(2) A watch worth £500 to celebrate Giles having worked for the company for 20 years.

(3) A newspaper allowance of £20 per month.

Giles receives no income other than employment income.

Required

The total taxable benefits for 2025/26 are:

£ [ ]

Task 3.16

Rita, a fashion designer for Daring Designs Ltd, was relocated from London to Manchester on 6 April 2025. Her annual salary is £48,000. She was reimbursed relevant relocation expenditure of £12,000. She was immediately provided with a house with an annual value of £4,000, for which her employer paid an annual rent of £3,500. Rita's employer provided ancillary services for the house in 2025/26 as follows:

	£
Electricity	700

	£
Gas	1,200
Water	500
Council tax	1,300
Property repairs	3,500

The house had been furnished by Daring Designs Ltd immediately prior to Rita's occupation, at a cost of £30,000. On 6 October 2025 Rita bought all of the furniture from Daring Designs Ltd for £20,000 when its market value was £25,000.

Daring Designs Limited had made an interest-free loan to Rita in 2023 of £10,000. No part of the loan has been repaid. Assume the official rate of interest is 3.75%.

Required

(a) The taxable benefit arising in respect of the accommodation provided for Rita in 2025/26 and purchase of the furniture is:

£ [ ]

(b) The taxable benefit arising in respect of the relocation expenses is:

£ [ ]

(c) The taxable benefit arising in respect of the interest free loan in 2025/26 is:

£ [ ]

Task 3.17

Jon's employer provided him with a flat throughout 2025/26. The employer had bought the flat for £99,750 on 1 April 2022. The annual value of the flat is £800. Jon pays £100 a month to his employer for the use of the flat.

Required

Tick to show the total taxable accommodation benefit for 2025/26.

	✓
£800	
£1,728	
£528	
£928	

Task 3.18

Petra uses her own car for business travel and her employer reimburses her 35p per mile. In 2025/26 Petra drove 13,000 business miles.

Required

Tick to show what is Petra's taxable benefit or allowable expense in respect of the business mileage.

	✓
Taxable benefit of £700	
Allowable expense of £700	
Allowable expense of £1,300	
Taxable benefit of £4,550	

Task 3.19

For an employee on an annual salary of £27,000, tick for each of the following benefits whether they would be taxable or exempt in 2025/26:

Item	Taxable ✓	Exempt ✓
Interest on loan of £2,000 (only loan provided)		
Removal costs of £6,000		
Use of pool car		
Reimbursement of business expenses		
One staff party costing £100 per head		
Accommodation provided to employee who is not required to live in it for the performance of employment		
Provision of parking space at work		
Additional costs of home working of £6 per week		
Non-cash long service award of £800 for 22 years of service		
Accommodation provided to a caretaker for proper performance of his employment duties		
Work related training		
Provision of second mobile phone		

Task 3.20

Selina is employed by JKL Ltd. She gives you the following information about money she has received from her employer, and expenditure that she has incurred in relation to her employment in 2025/26:

(1) Annual salary £30,000

(2) Reimbursed business expenses of £600

(3) Employee's contribution of 8% of salary to company's occupational pension scheme

(4) Membership of professional body of £150 paid by Selina

(5) Membership of fitness club of £300 paid by Selina – she often uses the club to meet new clients

(6) £50 donation to charity each month under the payroll deduction scheme

(7) £1,500 expenditure on smart clothes to wear to client meetings

(8) A mobile telephone which Selina uses to speak to clients only.

Required

Using the proforma layout provided, compute Selina's employment income for 2025/26. If an expense is not allowable or a payment is non-taxable enter 0. Both brackets and minus signs can be used to indicate negative numbers (the expenses). Fill in all of the unshaded boxes.

	£
Salary	
Less allowable expenses:	
reimbursed expenses	
pension contribution	
professional body membership	
fitness club membership	
charitable donation	
clothing	
Mobile telephone	
Employment income 2025/26	

Task 3.21

Lewis is required by his employer to move from Truro to Manchester.

Required

The maximum amount of relocation expenses that his employer can pay without a taxable benefit arising is:

£ [ ]

Task 3.22

In 2025/26 Dave earns £20,000 a year in his employment with BCD plc, and also receives dividend income of £6,300 from the company.

Required

Tick to show the maximum pension contribution that Dave can make in 2025/26, on which he can obtain tax relief.

	✓
£3,600	
£20,000	
£26,300	
£25,800	

Task 3.23

Zara works for KJ Ltd. She incurs the following travelling expenses in 2025/26:

	£
Travel from her home in Preston to her workplace in Manchester	1,500
Travel to meet clients	300
Travel from her home in Preston to a temporary workplace in Birmingham (temporary period is 18 months)	1,800

Required

Zara's qualifying travel expenses for 2025/26 are:

£ [ ]

Task 3.24

Tick to show how the payroll deduction scheme for occupational pensions works.

	✓
The employer deducts the contribution after calculating income tax under PAYE.	
The employer deducts basic rate tax from the contribution and the employee gets higher rate relief by extending the basic rate band in the tax computation.	
The employer deducts the contribution before calculating income tax under PAYE.	
The employer deducts basic rate tax from the contribution and there is no higher rate tax relief.	

Task 3.25

Tick to show how tax relief is given on an employee's charitable donations made via Payroll Giving.

	✓
The donation is paid net of basic rate tax, and higher rate tax relief is obtained by extending the basic rate band.	
The donation is deducted from employment income as an allowable expense before tax is calculated under PAYE.	

Task 3.26

This style of task is human marked in the live assessment.

You have received the following email from your client Martin Wilkes:

To:	MartinWilkes@boxmail.net
From:	AATStudent@boxmail.net
Date:	12 March 2026 10:24
Subject:	Car

I have just received a promotion, and my employer is offering me a brand-new company car for business and personal use from 6 April 2026. My employer is getting a good deal on the car because I looked up the list price, which is £18,000, but they are only paying £14,000 after a discount from the dealer. I also noted that the car has CO_2 emissions of 137 g/km.

My employer will pay all the running costs of the car and will also provide all the fuel. I will pay £20 a month towards private fuel, but I think that my actual private fuel used would cost about £50.

Can you please explain all of the taxation aspects of the provision of this car as a taxable benefit? Is there any other information that you need to know?

Thanks,

Martin Wilkes

Required

Reply to Martin's email, explaining to him the various taxation aspects that can apply to the provision of the car. Assume rates stay unchanged for future years.

To: AATStudent@boxmail.net

From: MartinWilkes@boxmail.net

Date: 14 March 2026 12:29

Subject: Car

Chapter 4 – Property income

Task 4.1

Simran rents out a furnished house from 1 July 2025. The rent is £500 per month, payable on the first day of each month. She has chosen to use the accrual basis for her property profits. She incurs the following costs relating to the rental:

	£
Electricity for 1 July 2025 to 31 March 2026	1,200
Water rates for 1 July 2025 to 31 March 2026	500
Insurance for 1 July 2025 to 30 June 2026	360
Replacement furniture purchased on 1 August 2025	400

Required

Tick to show what Simran's property income for 2025/26 is.

	✓
£2,630	
£2,540	
£2,040	
£2,130	

Task 4.2

Julie received the following property income during 2025/26:

(1) Annual rental of £6,300 (payable in advance) from a furnished flat first let on 6 August 2025. During the tax year the Julie spent £420 on replacement furniture and allowable expenses of £660.

(2) £3,500 from renting out her garage in London for parking.

Required

What amount of taxable property income does Julie have for 2025/26?

£ [ ]

Task 4.3

Zelda lets out a house and uses the accrual basis to calculate her profits. Her accrued income and allowable expenses are as follows:

	Income £	Expenses £
2023/24	6,000	10,000
2024/25	8,000	5,500
2025/26	10,000	4,000

Required

Zelda's property income for 2025/26 is:

£ [ ]

Task 4.4

On 1 October 2025 Nitin buys a badly dilapidated house for £350,000. During October 2025, he spends £40,000 on making the house habitable. He lets it, fully furnished, for £3,600 a month from 1 November 2025, but the tenant leaves on 31 January 2026. A new tenant moves in on 1 March 2026, paying £4,000 a month rent.

Water rates are £195 for the period 1 October 2025 to 31 March 2026, payable by Nitin. He also pays buildings insurance of £480 for the period from 1 October 2025 to 30 September 2026. He spends £1,461 on replacement carpets in February 2026. Nitin uses the accrual basis to calculate his property profits.

Required

Nitin's property income for 2025/26 is:

£ [ ]

Task 4.5

Sinead starts to let out property on 1 July 2025.

(1) On 1 July 2025, she lets a house which she has owned for several years. The tenant is required to pay annual rent of £8,000, quarterly in advance. The house is let unfurnished. She incurs total allowable expenses of £1,200 in relation to this letting.

(2) On 1 December 2025, she lets out a house which she has bought. The tenant pays rent of £450 per month, payable on the first of each month. The house is let unfurnished. She incurs total allowable expenses of £2,000 in relation to this letting.

Required

Sinead's property income for 2025/26 is:

£ [ ]

Task 4.6

In 2025/26, Sally makes a property income loss of £(5,000) on letting out Red Roofs, and property income profit of £3,000 on letting out Green Acres. Sally also has employment income of £20,000 in 2025/26.

Required

Sally can obtain loss relief by: (tick ONE box)

	✓
Setting the loss of £(5,000) against her employment income in 2025/26	
Carrying forward the loss of £(5,000) against property income in 2026/27	
Setting the loss of £(5,000) first against the profit of £3,000 in 2025/26 and then carrying forward the balance of £(2,000) against property income in 2026/27	
Setting the loss of £(5,000) first against the profit of £3,000 in 2025/26 and then setting the balance of £(2,000) against employment income in 2025/26	

Task 4.7

Pierce Jones owns a flat that he rents out for £500 per calendar month, payable on the first day of each month. The property is let furnished. His other expenses for 2025/26 were

	£
Electricity and gas	1,200
Water rates	400
Purchase of a television (not a replacement)	1,300
Repairs to roof following storm damage	3,200
Insurance	250

Required

What is his assessable property income for 2025/26?

£ [ ]

Task 4.8

(a) **Property income is assessed as: (tick ONE box)**

	✓
Non-savings income	
Savings income	
Dividend income	
Not taxable	

(b) **Property income is taxed at: (tick ONE box)**

	✓
20/40/45%	
10/20/40/45%	
0/8.75/33.75/39.35%	
0/20/40/45%	

Chapter 5 – National insurance

Task 5.1

In 2025/26 Steve received the following from his employer. For each item, indicate whether it would be subject to Class 1 Employee, Class 1 Employer, Class 1A National Insurance or none of these by ticking all the boxes that apply:

	Class 1 Employee ✓	Class 1 Employer ✓	Class 1A ✓	None ✓
Salary				
Company car				
Mileage expenses paid at 35p per mile				
Bonus				
Department store vouchers				
Reimbursed travel expenses				
Private gym membership				

Task 5.2

In 2025/26 Iain received the following from his employer. Salary £27,000 (paid monthly), company car £3,000 taxable benefit, bonus in December 2025 of £2,000.

Required

Show the national insurance that would be payable on these amounts.

(a) Class 1 Employee

£ [ ]

(b) Class 1 Employer

£ [ ]

(c) Class 1A

£ [ ]

Task 5.3

Ann was paid an annual salary of £45,000 in 2025/26 and her employer provided her with a laptop for personal use only. The taxable benefit for use of the laptop would be £300.

Required

Please complete the following sentence using the picklists below.

Ann and her employer would be liable to [(1) ▼] on [(2) ▼] and [(1) ▼] on [(2) ▼].

Picklist 1

- Class 1 Employee

- Class 1 Employee and Employer
- Class 1 Employer
- Class 1A

Picklist 2

- £300
- £45,000
- £45,300
- £nil

Task 5.4

Tick to show whether the following statement is true or false.

50p per mile paid to an employee for mileage would be exempt from national insurance.

	✓
True	
False	

Task 5.5

Tick to show whether the following statement is true or false.

Class 1A NIC is payable on vouchers given to an employee as a reward for working overtime.

	✓
True	
False	

Task 5.6

Wise Ltd has one employee, Freya, who is also a director of the company. In 2025/26 Wise Ltd pays Freya an annual salary of £37,000.

Required

What are the Class 1 employer contributions payable by Wise Ltd for 2025/26?

Please tick ONE box only.

	✓
£nil	
£5,550	
£4,800	
£3,665	

Task 5.7

What national insurance contributions are payable by employers and employees on a company car benefit? Please choose from the picklist below:

Employers	▼
Employees	▼

Picklist

- Class 1 Employee
- Class 1 Employer
- Class 1A
- None

Chapter 6 – Chargeable gains

Task 6.1

Fill in the boxes.

For the gain on the disposal of a capital asset to be a chargeable gain there must be a chargeable

[ ]

of a chargeable

[ ]

by a chargeable

[ ]

Task 6.2

Tick to show whether the following assets are chargeable assets or exempt assets for capital gains tax.

Item	Chargeable asset ✓	Exempt asset ✓
Car		
A plot of land		
Jewellery		
Premium bonds		
Government stock ('gilts')		

Task 6.3

Tick to show which ONE of the following is not a chargeable disposal for capital gains purposes.

	✓
The gift of an asset	
The sale of part of an asset	
The transfer of an asset on death	
The sale of the whole of an asset	

Task 6.4

Kate purchased a freehold property for £40,000. Kate then spent £5,000 on a new roof for the property as the old roof was storm damaged prior to acquisition. She sold the property for £90,100 on 15 March 2026. Kate had not made any other disposals during 2025/26.

Required

What is Kate's taxable gain for 2025/26?

	✓
£42,100	
£47,100	
£45,100	
£50,100	

Task 6.5

In November 2025, Lenny made chargeable gains of £17,400 and allowable losses of £3,560. He made no other disposals during 2025/26 and is a higher rate taxpayer.

Required

(a) Lenny's capital gains tax liability for 2025/26 is:

£ [ ]

(b) Lenny's capital gains tax liability is payable by: (insert date as XX/XX/XXXX)

[ ]

Task 6.6

In November 2025, Larry made chargeable gains of £22,400 and allowable losses of £5,200. He made no other disposals during 2025/26. He has £4,000 of his basic rate tax band remaining.

Required

Larry's capital gains tax liability for 2025/26 is:

£ [ ]

Task 6.7

Laura made chargeable gains of £5,400 in July 2025 and £14,500 in November 2025. In May 2025 she made allowable losses of £2,000. Laura has taxable income of £32,635 for 2025/26.

Required

Laura's capital gains tax liability for 2025/26 is:

£ [ ]

Task 6.8

Lisa made chargeable gains of £25,000 in December 2025. She made no other disposals in the year. Her taxable income for 2025/26 was £31,735.

Required

Lisa's capital gains tax liability for 2025/26 is:

£ [ ]

Task 6.9

Darren bought a 3-acre plot of land for £150,000. He sold two acres of the land at auction for £240,000. His disposal costs were £3,000. The market value of the one remaining acre at the date of sale was £60,000.

Required

(a) The cost of the land sold is:

£ [ ]

(b) The chargeable gain on sale is:

£ [ ]

Task 6.10

Tick to show how a taxpayer will pay the capital gains tax due for 2025/26.

	✓
The full amount will be paid on 31 January 2027	
The full amount will be paid on 31 January 2026	
Payments on account will be made on 31 January and 31 July 2026, with the balance being paid on 31 January 2027	
Payments on account will be made on 31 January and 31 July 2025, with the balance being paid on 31 January 2026	

Task 6.11

Mattheus made gains of £17,100 and losses of £7,000 in 2025/26. He has losses brought forward of £15,000.

Required

The losses to carry forward to 2026/27 are (do not use brackets or a minus sign):

£ [ ]

Task 6.12

Mike inherited a valuable painting from a distant uncle in November 2011. The painting had cost his uncle £5,000 in January 2003 and was valued at £9,000 at the date of his death. Luckily for Mike, when he sold it in December 2025, the proceeds were £16,000.

Required

Mike's chargeable gain on sale is:

£ [ ]

Task 6.13

Luke sells one acre of land in August 2025 for £25,000. His disposal costs were £2,500. He had bought four acres of land for £15,000. The market value of the remaining land was £50,000 at the date of sale. The acquisition costs of the four acres of land were £1,500.

Required

Luke's chargeable gain on sale is:

£ [ ]

Task 6.14

Tick to show whether the following statement is True or False.

If an individual has allowable losses brought forward, these are set off after the annual exempt amount.

	✓
True	
False	

Task 6.15

James has the following gains and losses arising from disposals of chargeable assets:

Tax year	2023/24	2024/25	2025/26
Gains	£2,000	£4,000	£14,000
Losses	£(14,000)	£(2,000)	£(2,000)

Required

The maximum allowable loss carried forward to 2026/27 will be:

£ [ ]

Task 6.16

Mary is married to Mike. They have a daughter, Beatrice. Mike has a sister, Susan who is married to Simon. Susan and Simon have a daughter called Sarah.

Required

Tick which ONE of the following is not a connected person in relation to Mary.

	✓
Beatrice	
Susan	
Simon	
Sarah	

Task 6.17

Joanne gives an asset to her son in September 2025. There was an allowable loss on the disposal of £(3,000). Joanne also gave an asset to her daughter in October 2025. There was a chargeable gain of £5,000 on this disposal.

Required

Tick to show whether the following statement is True or False.

The loss of £(3,000) can be set against the gain of £5,000.

	✓
True	
False	

Task 6.18

Xena bought a vase for £1,500 and sold it in October 2025 for £6,500, incurring expenses of sale of £130.

Required

Her chargeable gain on sale is:

£ [ ]

Task 6.19

Jolyon purchased a gold ring for £7,000. He sold it in January 2026 for £3,000. The expenses of sale were £125.

Required

Jolyon's allowable loss is (do not use brackets or a minus sign):

£ [ ]

Task 6.20

Rowenna bought a necklace for £4,000. She sold it in September 2025 for £5,500.

Required

Tick to show whether the following statement is True or False.

Rowenna has a chargeable gain on sale of £1,500.

	✓
True	
False	

Task 6.21

Gilda purchased a picture for £3,500 and sold it in September 2025 for £7,500, incurring £300 expenses of sale.

Required

Tick to show the chargeable gain on sale of the picture.

	✓
£1,200	
£2,200	
£2,500	
£3,700	

Task 6.22

Mark purchased an antique vase for £9,000. He sold the vase in August 2025 at auction for £4,500 net of auctioneer's fees of £500.

Required

Mark's allowable loss is (both minus signs and brackets can be used to indicate negative numbers):

£ [ ]

Chapter 7 – Share disposals

Task 7.1

On 17 January 2026 Lionel sold 10,000 ordinary shares in Old plc. He had originally purchased 12,000 shares in Old plc on 10 May 2010 and purchased another 8,000 shares on 24 January 2026.

Required

Tick to show how Lionel's disposal of 10,000 shares in Old plc will be matched with his acquisitions.

	✓
Against 10,000 of the shares purchased on 10 May 2010	
Against 5,000 of the shares purchased on 24 January 2026 and then against 5,000 of the shares purchased on 10 May 2010	
Against 10,000 of the total shareholding of 20,000 shares	
Against the 8,000 shares purchased on 24 January 2026 and then against 2,000 of the shares purchased on 10 May 2010	

Task 7.2

Mr Stevens sold 5,000 ordinary shares in JKL plc for £20,000 on 10 August 2025. He bought 6,000 shares in JKL plc for £9,000 on 15 July 2020 and another 1,000 shares for £4,200 on 16 August 2025.

Required

His net chargeable gain on sale is:

£ ________

Task 7.3

This style of task is human marked in the live assessment.

Eloise's dealings in Moo plc were as follows:

	No. of shares	Cost/proceeds £
10 February 2003	12,000	18,000
20 September 2010	Bonus issue of 1 for 4	Nil
15 March 2026	(2,000)	8,000

Required

Using the proforma layout provided, calculate Eloise's gain on sale. Fill in all the unshaded boxes and if the answer is zero insert '0'. Both minus signs and brackets can be used to indicate negative numbers.

Share pool

	No. of shares	Cost £
10 February 2003		
20 September 2010 Bonus 1:4		
15 March 2026 Disposal		

Gain on sale

	£
Proceeds	
Less cost	
Gain	

Task 7.4

This style of task is human marked in the live assessment.

Mark sold 10,000 of his shares in AC plc on 4 November 2025 for £60,000. The shares had been acquired as follows:

	No. of shares	Cost £
9 December 2003	12,000	4,400
12 October 2007 (Rights issue 1:3 at £5)		
10 November 2025	2,000	11,500

Required

Calculate Mark's total chargeable gain on sale. All workings must be shown. If the answer is zero insert '0'. Both minus signs and brackets can be used to indicate negative numbers.

Task 7.5

This style of task is human marked in the live assessment.

Darren sold 700,000 of his shares in R plc on 24 September 2025 for £3,675,000. The shares had been acquired as follows:

	No. of shares	Cost £
2 June 2008	500,000	960,000
1 December 2013 (Bonus issue 3:2)		

Required

Calculate Darren's total chargeable gain on sale. All workings must be shown. If the answer is zero insert '0'. Both minus signs and brackets can be used to indicate negative numbers.

Chapter 8 – Private residence relief

Task 8.1

Nicole is selling her main residence, which she has owned for 25 years. She lived in the house for the first eight years and nine months of ownership, let the property for the next five years whilst she was posted abroad by her employer, returned to live in the house for the next two years, and then moved out for the remainder of her period of ownership.

Required

Tick to show what fraction of her gain will be exempt under the private residence exemption.

	✓
16.5/25	
10.75/25	
15.75/25	
8.5/25	

Task 8.2

Mr Kitch bought a house in 2010 and lived in it until June 2025 when he moved out to live with his girlfriend. He sold the house in December 2025 and made a gain of £30,000.

Required

The whole gain will be covered by private residence relief.

	✓
True	
False	

Task 8.3

Mr Fox bought a house on 1 August 2005 for £50,000. He lived in the house until 31 July 2008. He then went abroad to work as a self-employed engineer until 31 July 2013. He lived in the house again until 31 January 2014, when he moved out.

Mr Fox sold the house on 31 July 2025 for £180,000.

Required

Using the proforma layout provided, calculate the chargeable gain on sale.

	£
Proceeds	
Less cost	
Gain before private residence exemption	
Less private residence exemption	
Chargeable gain	

QUESTIONS

Task 8.4

Jose purchased a house and lived in it for three years. The house was then unoccupied for five years when he was required to work abroad in Spain. He moved back to the UK and lived in the house for two years before moving out to live with his girlfriend. The house was unoccupied for four years before he moved back to the house for the final six months of ownership.

Required

Tick to show what fraction of his gain will be exempt under the private residence exemption.

	✓
13.75/14.5	
13.5/14.5	
10.5/14.5	
10.75/14.5	

Task 8.5

David purchased a house in 2010. He lived in the property for a year before going travelling for four years. He moved back to the property for five years before going to work abroad for his current employer. He sold the house in 2025 without returning to the property.

Required

All periods of absence will be covered by private residence relief.

	✓
True	
False	

Chapter 9 – Inheritance tax

Task 9.1

Identify whether the following transfers will be treated as a PET or exempt for Inheritance Tax purposes in 2025/26. Tick ONE box per transfer.

	PET ✓	Exempt ✓
Gift of £100 cash to niece		
Gift of property which is rented out worth £100,000 to daughter		
Gift of £5,000 to son on the occasion of his marriage		
Gift of £25,000 to a friend		
Gift of classic car to spouse		

Task 9.2

Norman died in May 2025. His estate was valued at £500,000. £100,000 was left to his cousin and the balance to his wife Maureen. Neither Norman nor Maureen own any property.

Required

How much nil band would be available to Maureen on her death?

£ [ ]

Task 9.3

Identify which of the following debts would be deductible and which would not be deductible in a death estate?

	Deductible ✓	Not deductible ✓
Grocery bill		
HM Revenue & Customs – income tax to death		
Mortgage on home		
Illegal gambling debt		

Task 9.4

Tick to show whether the following statement is true or false.

PETs are subject to inheritance tax in both life and death.

	✓
True	
False	

QUESTIONS

Task 9.5

Tick to show whether the following statement is true or false.

A £5,000 exemption is available on any gifts given on a marriage.

	✓
True	
False	

Task 9.6

On 15 July 2025 Yvonne gave £500,000 to a trust for the benefit of her grandchildren. Yvonne died on 27 December 2025.

Required

What are the due dates for inheritance tax to be paid on this transfer of value? (please tick ONE box only)

Lifetime tax	Death tax	✓
31 January 2026	30 June 2026	
30 April 2026	30 June 2026	
31 January 2026	30 April 2026	
30 April 2026	30 April 2026	

Task 9.7

Bernard made a chargeable lifetime transfer of £420,000 to a trust for the benefit of his son and daughter in November 2025 (having made a chargeable lifetime transfer of £500,000 in August 2024). Bernard agreed to pay any lifetime IHT due.

Required

At what rate will IHT be payable?

	✓
0%	
20%	
25%	
40%	

Task 9.8

Kalila gave cash of £40,000 to her grandson in August 2020. She died in November 2025.

Required

What percentage taper relief is available when calculating the death tax on this gift?

[ ] %

Task 9.9

June gives 200 shares to her daughter – these shares are worth £3 each. June owned 500 shares prior to this transfer and the shares were worth £10 each. After the transfer June's remaining shares will be valued at £7.50 each.

Required

What is the diminution in value of June's estate?

£ ______

Task 9.10

Amanda gifted cash of £2,000 to her daughter in September 2025 and made a chargeable lifetime transfer of £6,000 in February 2026. She had not made any previous gifts.

Required

What is the amount of annual exemption that would be set against the February 2026 transfer?

Please tick ONE box only.

	✓
£6,000	
£4,000	
£3,000	
£1,000	

Chapter 10 – The tax and ethical framework

Task 10.1

The tax year 2025/26 runs from: (insert dates as XX/XX/XXXX)

until:

Task 10.2

Tick to show whether the following statement is true or false.

Detailed regulations relating to tax law are contained in Statutory Instruments.

	✓
True	
False	

Task 10.3

Tick to show who the UK tax system is administered by.

	✓
Parliament	
His Majesty's Revenue & Customs (HMRC)	
National Crime Agency (NCA)	
HM Customs & Excise	

Task 10.4

If you are employed by a firm of accountants, and suspect that one of your clients may be engaged in money laundering, whom should you inform about your suspicions?

	✓
HMRC	
Your firm's Money Laundering Reporting Officer	
National Crime Agency	
Tax Tribunal	

Task 10.5

This style of task is human marked in the live assessment.

One of your clients has expressed concern that his personal tax information may be disclosed to members of his family, who are also clients of your firm. He feels that this would compromise his right to privacy in his personal affairs.

Required

Write a note responding to this concern.

Task 10.6

Tick to show in which TWO of the following situations an accountant is able to disclose information about a client without their permission.

	✓
If the client is unwell and unable to respond to HMRC	
If money laundering is suspected	
Where it would be illegal not to disclose the information	
If the information is requested from a 'connected person'	

Task 10.7

The five fundamental principles of professional ethics for AAT members are:

Use the letters in the left column as a guide.

I	
O	
Pc and dc	
C	
Pb	

Task 10.8

Tick to show who you should inform about your suspicions if you are a sole practitioner and suspect that one of your clients may be engaged in money laundering.

	✓
HMRC	
Another firm's Money Laundering Reporting Officer	
National Crime Agency	
Tax Tribunal	

QUESTIONS

Task 10.9

Tick to show whether the following statement is true or false.

A non-UK resident individual is liable to pay income tax on their UK and overseas income.

	✓
True	
False	

Task 10.10

This style of task is human marked in the live assessment.

A client has received a tax refund of £12,000 from HMRC. They were not due this refund but have already spent the money and asked you not to inform HMRC of their mistake.

Required

What action should you take?

Task 10.11

Tick to show whether the following statement is true or false.

Tax avoidance is illegal.

	✓
True	
False	

Answers

Chapter 1 – Taxable income

Task 1.1

	Non-savings income ✓	Savings income ✓	Dividend income ✓
Trading income	✓		
Dividend received from a company			✓
Property income	✓		
Building society interest		✓	
Bank interest		✓	
Pension income	✓		
Employment income	✓		
Interest from government stock ('gilts')		✓	

Task 1.2

(a) £ 160

(b) £ 0

Premium bond prizes are exempt income.

(c) £ 540

Task 1.3

	Gross ✓	Net ✓	Exempt ✓
Bank interest	✓		
Interest on an individual savings account (ISA)			✓
Employment income		✓	
Interest from government stock ('gilts')	✓		

Task 1.4

£ 26,373

	Non-savings income £	Savings income £	Dividend income £	Total £
Earnings	38,800			

ANSWERS

	Non-savings income £	Savings income £	Dividend income £	Total £
Building society interest		80		
Dividends			63	
Net income	38,800	80	63	38,943
Less personal allowance	(12,570)			(12,570)
Taxable income	26,230	80	63	26,373

Task 1.5

	Non-savings income £	Savings income £	Total £
Earnings	15,665	0	
Bank deposit interest	0	457	
Building society interest	0	400	
ISA interest	0	0	
Net income	15,665	857	16,522
Less personal allowance	(12,570)	0	(12,570)
Taxable income	3,095	857	3,952

Task 1.6

(a) £ 101,100

	Non-savings income £	Savings income £	Dividend income £	Total £
Employment income	95,000			
Bank interest		1,600		
Dividends			4,500	
Net income	95,000	1,600	4,500	101,100

Note. ISA interest is exempt from income tax.

(b) £ 12,020

	£
Net income	101,100
Less income limit	(100,000)
Excess	1,100
Personal allowance	12,570
Less half excess	(550)
	12,020

Task 1.7

£ 6,570

	£
Net income	116,000
Less Gift Aid donations (gross)	(4,000)
Adjusted net income	112,000
Less income limit	(100,000)
Excess	12,000
Personal allowance	12,570
Less half excess	(6,000)
	6,570

Task 1.8

(a) £ 26,700

	Non-savings income £	Savings income £	Dividend income £	Total £
Pension income	19,300			
Bank interest		2,000		
Dividends			5,400	
Net income	19,300	2,000	5,400	26,700

Note. Lottery winnings are exempt from income tax.

(b) £ 12,570

Task 1.9

£ 20,000

Task 1.10

The correct answer is:

	✓
True	✓
False	

Task 1.11

The correct answer is:

	✓
True	
False	✓

The statement is false. Damages received for both injury and death are always exempt from income tax.

Chapter 2 – Calculation of income tax

Task 2.1

(a) £ 1,356

	Non-savings income £	Savings income £	Total £
Non-savings income	12,850		
Bank interest		7,500	
Net Income	12,850	7,500	20,350
PA	(12,570)		(12,570)
Taxable income	280	7,500	7,780
Tax:			
NSI £280 × 20%		56	
SI £1,000 × 0% (PSA)		0	
SI £7,500 –1,000 = £6,500 × 20%		1,300	
Income tax liability		1,356	

(b) £ 10,972

	Non-savings income £	Savings income £	Total £
Non-savings income	51,850		
Interest		7,500	
Net income	51,850	7,500	59,350
PA	(12,570)		(12,570)
Taxable income	39,280	7,500	46,780
Tax:			
NSI £37,700 × 20%		7,540	
NSI £39,280 – 37,700 = £1,580 × 40%		632	
SI £500 × 0% (PSA)		0	
SI £7,500 – 500 = £7,000 × 40%		2,800	
Income tax liability		10,972	

Task 2.2

Note. that 'taxable income' is the figure after the personal allowance.

	Non-savings income £	Savings income £	Dividend income £	Total £
Taxable income	14,700	2,176	1,266	18,142
Tax on non-savings income:	£14,700 × 20%		2,940	
Tax on savings income:				
£1,000 Basic Rate PSA	£1,000 × 0%		0	
Balance of savings income	£1,176 × 20%		235	
Tax on dividend income:				
£500 DA	£500 × 0%		0	
Balance of dividend income	£766 × 8.75%		67	
Income tax liability			3,242	

(a) £ 2,940

(b) £ 235

(c) £ 67

Task 2.3

The correct answer is:

	✓
£125,140	
£137,140	
£140,140	✓
£128,140	

Additional rate threshold £125,140 plus gross personal pension contribution of £15,000 (£12,000 × 100/80) = £140,140

The answer of £125,140 is the additional rate threshold without adjustment. The answer £137,140 does not gross up the pension contribution. The answer £128,140 only adjusts the limit for the difference between the gross and net pension contribution.

Task 2.4

The correct answer is:

	✓
£43,700	
£37,700	
£45,200	✓
£30,200	

Basic rate band extended by the gross Gift Aid donation, ie £(6,000 × 100/80) = £7,500

£37,700 + £7,500 = £45,200

The answer £43,700 does not gross up the Gift Aid donation. The answer £37,700 is the basic rate threshold without adjustment. The answer £30,200 deducts the Gift Aid donation.

Task 2.5

(a) **£** 42,700

Basic rate band extended by the gross Gift Aid donation, ie £(4,000 × 100/80) = £5,000

£37,700 + £5,000

(b) £ 130,140

Additional rate threshold = £125,140 + £5,000

(c) £ 87,440

(£130,140 – £42,700)

Task 2.6

(a) £ 1,000

Ruth is a basic rate taxpayer with ANI of <£50,270 (£37,700 + £12,570)

(b) £ 500

The £500 dividend allowance is applicable to all taxpayers regardless of their marginal rate of tax.

Task 2.7

£ 2,170

Net income	24,420
Less personal allowance	(12,570)
Taxable income	11,850
£1,000 × 0% (PSA)	0
£11,850 – 1,000 = £10,850 × 20%	2,170

Income tax liability	2,170

Task 2.8

£ 3,470

'Taxable income' is the figure after personal allowances have been deducted.

	£
Taxable income	58,525

	£
Tax £37,700 × 20%	7,540
£13,500 (extended by £10,800 × 100/80) × 20%	2,700
£51,200	
£7,325 × 40%	2,930
£58,525	
Income tax liability	13,170
Less tax suffered at source (PAYE)	(9,700)
Income tax payable	3,470

Task 2.9

(a)

	Non-savings income £	Savings income £	Dividend income £	Total £
Salary	50,850	0	0	
Dividend	0	0	500	
Bank deposit interest	0	800	0	
Net income	50,850	800	500	52,150
Less personal allowance	(12,570)	0	0	(12,570)
Taxable income	38,280	800	500	39,580

The gross Gift Aid payment is £2,400 × 100/80 = £3,000.

The adjusted net income (52,150 – 3,000 Gift Aid) is less than £50,270 and so the £1,000 PSA applies. The alternative logic is that the basic rate band is extended to £40,700 (£37,700 + £3,000) which is greater than the amount of taxable income.

(b) £ 7,656

(c) £ 86

	£
Tax on non-savings income	
£37,700 × 20%	7,540
£580 × 20%	116
Gift aid extended the basic rate band to £37,700 + £3,000 (£2,400 × 100/80) = £40,700	
Tax on savings income	
£800 × 0% (PSA £1,000)	0
Tax on dividend income	
£500 × 0% (covered by DA)	0
Income tax liability	7,656
Less PAYE (given)	(7,570)
Income tax payable	86

Task 2.10

(a)

	Non-savings income £	Savings income £	Dividend income £	Total £
Salary	155,000	0	0	
Dividend	0	0	10,000	
Bank deposit interest	0	3,000	0	
Net income	155,000	3,000	10,000	168,000
Less personal allowance	0	0	0	0
Taxable income	155,000	3,000	10,000	168,000

The adjusted net income is in excess of £125,140 so the personal allowance is reduced to nil.

Additional rate threshold is increased by the gross personal pension contribution £10,000 (£8,000 × 100/80) to £135,140. Jean is not entitled to a personal savings allowance as she is an additional rate taxpayer.

(b) £ 58,541

(c) £ 10,041

ANSWERS

	£
Tax on non-savings income	
£37,700 × 20%	7,540
£10,000 (extended band: pension) £8,000 × 100/80 × 20%	2,000
£87,440 × 40%	34,976
£135,140 (extended higher rate band £125,140 + £10,000)	
£19,860 × 45%	8,937
Tax on savings income	
£3,000 × 45%	1,350
Tax on dividend income	
£500 × 0% (DA)	0
£9,500 × 39.35%	3,738
Income tax liability	58,541
Less tax deducted at source	
PAYE (given)	(48,500)
Income tax payable	10,041

Task 2.11

	Non-savings income £	Savings income £	Dividend income £	Total £
Pension income	10,050			
Bank interest		11,145		
Dividends			9,500	
Net income	10,050	11,145	9,500	30,695
Personal allowance	(10,050)	(2,520)		(12,570)
Taxable income	Nil	8,625	9,500	18,125
Tax on savings income:				
£1,000 × 0% (PSA)		0		
£7,625 (£8,625 – £1,000) × 20%		1,525		
Tax on dividend income:				
£500 × 0% (DA)		0		
£9,000 × 8.75%		788		
Income tax liability		2,313		

Adjusted net income ≤ £50,270 hence £1,000 PSA available.

Basic rate taxpayer therefore correct relief given at source so Gift Aid payment ignored.

Task 2.12

	Non-savings income £	Savings income £	Dividend income £	Total £
Trading income	90,000			
Bank interest		1,500		
Dividends			15,000	
Net income	90,000	1,500	15,000	106,500
Personal allowance (W)	(9,320)			(9,320)
Taxable income	80,680	1,500	15,000	97,180
Tax on non-savings income:		£		
£37,700 × 20%		7,540		
£42,980 × 40%		17,192		
Tax on savings income:				
£500 × 0% (PSA)		0		
£1,000 × 40%		400		
Tax on dividend income:				
£500 × 0% (DA)		0		
£14,500 × 33.75%		4,894		
Income tax liability		30,026		

(W) Jack has adjusted net income of £106,500 and therefore his personal allowance is restricted to: 12,570 – ((106,500 – 100,000) / 2) = £9,320.

Note. Jack is a higher rate taxpayer and therefore only receives £500 PSA.

Chapter 3 – Employment income

Task 3.1

The correct answer is:

	✓
True	
False	✓

An employee has a contract of service.

Task 3.2

The correct answers are:

Factor	Contract of service ✓	Contract for services ✓
Peter is entitled to paid holidays	✓	
Peter hires his own helpers		✓
Peter takes substantial financial risks when undertaking work for XYZ plc		✓
Peter does not have to rectify mistakes in his work at his own expense	✓	

Task 3.3

Item	£
Salary	24,280
Commission	0
Employer's pension contribution	0
Bonus	1,200

Salary paid on the first of each month, therefore received in 2025/26 as follows:

1 May 2025 to 1 September 2025 = 5 × £2,000 = £10,000

1 October 2025 to 1 April 2026 = 7 × £2,000 × 102% = £14,280

Salary = £10,000 + £14,280 = £24,280

Task 3.4

The correct answer is:

	✓
True	
False	✓

Tips received by a tour guide from customers are earnings. Note that earnings can include money received other than from the employer.

Task 3.5

20/12/2025

Task 3.6

(a) £ 15,000

(b) 34 %

The CO_2 emissions of the car are 140g/km (rounded down to the nearest five).

Amount over baseline figure: 140 – 55 = 85 g/km

Divide 5 by 5 = 17

The taxable percentage is 17% + 17% = 34%

(c) £ 3,400

34% × £15,000 × 8/12 (6 August 2025 to 5 April 2026)

Task 3.7

(a) £ 6,525

Round down CO_2 emissions to 135g/km

Amount above baseline: 135 – 55 = 80g/km

Divide 80 by 5 = 16

Taxable % = 17% + 16% = 33%

	£
£25,000 × 33% × 10/12	6,875
Less employee contribution (10 × £35)	(350)
Taxable benefit of car	6,525

(b) £ 7,755

£28,200 × 33% × 10/12 = £7,755

Task 3.8

(a) £ 11,500

(b) 20 %

Round down CO_2 emissions to 70g/km

Amount above baseline: 70 – 55 = 15g/km

Divide 15 by 5 = 3

Taxable % = 17% + 3% = 20%

(c) £ 5,640

£28,200 × 20%

Task 3.9

(a) The correct answer is:

	✓
27	
37	✓
17	
44	

Round down CO_2 emissions to 190 g/km

Amount above baseline: 190 – 55 = 135 g/km

Divide 135 by 5 = 27

Taxable % = 17% + 27% = 44%, max 37%

The answer 27% is the amount to add to the basic taxable percentage. The answer 17% is the basic percentage. The answer 44% ignores the maximum rate.

(b) £ 19,240

	£
List price	57,000
Less capital contribution paid by employee (max)	(5,000)
Cost of car	52,000
Car benefit £52,000 × 37%	19,240

(c) £ 10,434

£28,200 × 37% = £10,434. There is no reduction for part reimbursement of private fuel.

Task 3.10

The correct answer is:

	✓
£4,020	
£4,789	
£769	
Nil	✓

There is no taxable benefit because there is no private use of the van – travel from home to work is not private use for vans.

The answer £4,020 is the private use benefit. The answer £4,789 is the private use benefit plus the private use fuel benefit. The answer £769 is the private use fuel benefit.

Task 3.11

£ 110

The benefit taxable in 2024/25 was 20% × £200 = £40

The benefit taxable in 2025/26 will be the greater of:

		£	£
(1)	Market value at acquisition by employee	120	
(2)	Original market value	200	
	Less benefit for use in 2024/25	(40)	
		160	
	Greater		160
	Less price paid by employee		(50)
	Taxable benefit 2025/26		110

Task 3.12

(a) £ 775

	£
3.75% × (50,000 + 30,000)/2	1,500
Less interest paid	(725)
Taxable benefit	775

(b) £ 900

	£
£50,000 × 8/12 × 3.75%	1,250
(6 April 2025 to 5 December 2025)	
£30,000 × 4/12 × 3.75%	375
(6 December 2025 to 5 April 2026)	
	1,625
Less interest paid	(725)

ANSWERS

	£
Taxable benefit	900

Task 3.13

The correct answer is:

	✓
True	
False	✓

There is a taxable benefit of the amount of the loan written-off, however small the loan. The £10,000 limit only applies to the interest benefit.

Task 3.14

(a) £ 650

During 2025/26 Vimal will have a taxable benefit arising from the use of the asset:

£1,000 × 20% × 9/12 = £150

He will also have a benefit when the asset is sold to him at an undervalue.

This will be the higher of the MV at the date of the 'gift', and the original market value minus benefits assessed so far, less his £100 contribution.

	£	£
Market value at date of gift		300
Original market value		1,000
Assessed re use:		
2023/24: £1,000 × 20% × 3/12	50	
2024/25: £1,000 × 20%	200	
2025/26: £1,000 × 20% × 9/12	150	
		(400)
		600
Higher value used		600
Less Vimal's contribution		(100)
		500
His total benefit (for both use and 'gift') in 2025/26 will therefore be		650

(b) £ 5,109

The taxable benefit for use of the flat is calculated as follows:

	£
Annual value	3,000
£(131,250 – 75,000) × 3.75% (expensive accommodation)	2,109
Taxable benefit	5,109

The original cost is used, not the value now.

Task 3.15

£ 625

	£
Medical insurance (cost to employer)	385
Non-cash long service award (up to £50 × 20 years = £1,000)	0
Newspaper allowance (12 × £20)	240
Taxable benefits	625

Task 3.16

(a) £ 21,200

	£
Annual value (higher than rent paid)	4,000
Electricity	700
Gas	1,200
Water	500
Council tax	1,300
Repairs	3,500
Furniture (20% × £30,000 × 6/12)	3,000
Purchase of furniture (W)	7,000
	21,200

Working

Purchase of furniture

Benefit is the **higher** of:

		£
(1)	Cost	30,000
	Less taxed for use of furniture (20% × £30,000 × 6/12)	(3,000)
		27,000
	Less amount paid by Rita	(20,000)
		7,000
(2)	Market value	25,000
	Less amount paid	(20,000)
		5,000

(b) £ 4,000

£12,000 – £8,000

(c) £ Nil

No taxable benefit arises if the combined outstanding balance on all loans to the employee did not exceed £10,000 at any time in the tax year.

Task 3.17

The correct answer is:

	✓
£800	
£1,728	
£528	✓
£928	

	£
Annual value	800
Less contribution (£100 × 12 = £1,200)	(800)
	Nil

Additional charge

	£	£
Cost	99,750	
Less	(75,000)	

	£	£
Excess	24,750	
£24,750 × 3.75%		928
Less contribution (£1,200 – £800)		(400)
Total benefit 2025/26		528

The answer £800 is the annual value of the flat. The answer £1,728 (£800 + 928) ignores the contribution made by Jon. The answer £928 is the additional charge before adjusting for contribution made.

Task 3.18

The correct answer is:

	✓
Taxable benefit of £700	
Allowable expense of £700	✓
Allowable expense of £1,300	
Taxable benefit of £4,550	

	£	£
Amount received 13,000 × 35p		4,550
Less statutory amounts		
10,000 × 45p	4,500	
3,000 × 25p	750	
		(5,250)
Allowable expense		(700)

The answer taxable benefit of £700 treats the difference the wrong way round. The answer allowable expense of £1,300 calculates the statutory amounts all at 45p. The answer taxable benefit of £4,550 treats the entire receipt as a benefit.

Task 3.19

The correct answers are:

Item	Taxable ✓	Exempt ✓
Interest on loan of £2,000 (only loan provided)		✓
Removal costs of £6,000		✓
Use of pool car		✓
Reimbursement of business expenses		✓
One staff party costing £100 per head		✓

Item	Taxable ✓	Exempt ✓
Accommodation provided to employee who is not required to live in it for the performance of employment	✓	
Provision of parking space at work		✓
Additional costs of home working of £6 per week		✓
Non-cash long service award of £800 for 22 years of service		✓
Accommodation provided to a caretaker for proper performance of his employment duties		✓
Work related training		✓
Provision of second mobile phone	✓	

Task 3.20

	£
Salary	30,000
Less allowable expenses:	
reimbursed expenses	0
pension contribution	(2,400)
professional body membership	(150)
fitness club membership	0
charitable donation	(600)
clothing	0
Mobile telephone (exempt)	0
Employment income 2025/26	26,850

Task 3.21

£ 8,000

Task 3.22

The correct answer is:

	✓
£3,600	
£20,000	✓
£26,300	
£25,800	

The maximum contribution is the higher of £3,600 and his earnings of £20,000.

Dividends are not earnings.

The answer £3,600 is the statutory maximum contribution without earnings. The answer £26,300 treats dividend income as earnings. The answer £25,800 treats taxable dividend income as earnings (after the £500 dividend allowance).

Task 3.23

£ 2,100

£300 + £1,800. Travel expenses from home to a permanent workplace are not allowable.

Task 3.24

The correct answer is:

	✓
The employer deducts the contribution after calculating income tax under PAYE.	
The employer deducts basic rate tax from the contribution and the employee gets higher rate relief by extending the basic rate band in the tax computation.	
The employer deducts the contribution before calculating income tax under PAYE.	✓
The employer deducts basic rate tax from the contribution and there is no higher rate tax relief.	

The employer deducts the contribution before calculating income tax, so giving tax relief at the applicable rate/s.

Task 3.25

The correct answer is:

	✓
The donation is paid net of basic rate tax, and higher rate tax relief is obtained by extending the basic rate band.	
The donation is deducted from employment income as an allowable expense before tax is calculated under PAYE.	✓

Task 3.26

To: AATStudent@boxmail.net

From: MartinWilkes@boxmail.net

Date: 14 March 2026 12:29

Subject: Car

The car benefit is calculated as a percentage of the car's list price, not the actual price paid by the employer.

The percentage (that is multiplied by the list price) is dependent on the car's CO_2 emissions rating. For cars which emit CO_2 of 55g – 59/km the percentage is 17%, and then this

ANSWERS

percentage increases by 1% for every additional whole 5g/km of CO_2 emissions above 55g/km, up to a maximum of 37%.

In this case, the percentage would be 17% + 16% = 33%.

As the employer will be paying for fuel used for private motoring, a fuel benefit arises. The benefit is a percentage of £28,200. The percentage is the same percentage as is used to calculate the car benefit, ie 33% in this instance.

No benefit arises if you reimburse the whole of the expense of any fuel provided for private use, but there is no reduction to the benefit if only part of the expense for private use fuel is reimbursed, as here. It would be better for the contribution to be set against the use of the car, as this would be deductible in calculating the car benefit.

Chapter 4 – Property income

Task 4.1

The correct answer is:

	✓
£2,630	
£2,540	
£2,040	
£2,130	✓

	£
Rent received (9 months × £500 – accrual basis)	4,500
Less electricity	(1,200)
water rates	(500)
insurance 9/12 × £360	(270)
replacement furniture relief	(400)
Property income 2025/26	2,130

The answer £2,630 includes the rent received on 1 April which is not taxable under the accrual basis. The answer £2,540 is the cash basis. The answer £2,040 does not pro-rate insurance expenses ie uses cash basis.

Task 4.2

£ 8,720

	£
Rent received (cash basis)	6,300
Less expenses	(660)
Replacement furniture relief	(420)
Garage	3,500
Property income 2025/26	8,720

Task 4.3

£ 4,500

	£
2023/24	
Income	6,000

ANSWERS

	£
Expenses	(10,000)
Loss cfwd	(4,000)
2024/25	
Income	8,000
Expenses	(5,500)
	2,500
Less loss b/f	(2,500)
	Nil
Loss cfwd £1,500 (£4,000 – £2,500)	
2025/26	
Income	10,000
Expenses	(4,000)
	6,000
Less loss b/f	(1,500)
Taxable property income 2025/26	4,500

Task 4.4

£ 12,904

	£
Rent (£3,600 × 3)	10,800
Rent (£4,000 × 1)	4,000
	14,800
Less water rates	(195)
insurance (£480 × 6/12)	(240)
initial repairs: capital	0
replacement furniture relief	(1,461)
Property income 2025/26	12,904

Task 4.5

£ 7,050

	£
Property one: rent (4 × £2,000)	8,000
Property two: rent (5 × £450)	2,250
Less expenses on property one	(1,200)
expenses on property two	(2,000)
Property income 2025/26	7,050

Task 4.6

The correct answer is:

	✓
Setting the loss of £(5,000) against her employment income in 2025/26	
Carrying forward the loss of £(5,000) against property income in 2026/27	
Setting the loss of £(5,000) first against the profit of £3,000 in 2025/26 and then carrying forward the balance of £(2,000) against property income in 2026/27	✓
Setting the loss of £(5,000) first against the profit of £3,000 in 2025/26 and then setting the balance of £(2,000) against employment income in 2025/26	

Task 4.7

£ 950

	£
Rent (£500 × 12)	6,000
Rates and insurance (£400 + £250)	(650)
Roof repairs	(3,200)
Electricity and gas	(1,200)
Property income 2025/26	950

The television is not a deductible expense and does not qualify for replacement furniture relief.

Task 4.8

(a) The correct answer is:

	✓
Non-savings income	✓
Savings income	
Dividend income	
Not taxable	

ANSWERS

(b) The correct answer is:

	✓
20/40/45%	✓
10/20/40/45%	
0/8.75/33.75/39.35%	
0/20/40/45%	

Chapter 5 – National insurance

Task 5.1

	Class 1 Employee ✓	Class 1 Employer ✓	Class 1A ✓	None ✓
Salary	✓	✓		
Company car			✓	
Mileage expenses paid at 35p per mile				✓
Bonus	✓	✓		
Department store vouchers	✓	✓		
Reimbursed travel expenses				✓
Private gym membership			✓	

Task 5.2

(a) £ 1,310

(b) £ 3,599

(c) £ 450

Working

£27,000/12 months = £2,250 per month.

Employee		£
£(2,250 – 1,048) = 1,202 × 8% × 11 months	=	1,058
£(4,189 – 1,048) = 3,141 × 8% × 1 month	=	251
£(2,250 + £2,000 – 4,189) = 61 × 2% × 1 month	=	1
	=	1,310

Employer		£
£(2,250 – 417) = 1,833 × 15% × 11 months	=	3,024
£(2,250 + 2,000 – 417) = 3,833 × 15% × 1 month	=	575
	=	3,599
1A		
£3,000 × 15%	=	450

ANSWERS

Task 5.3

Ann and her employer would be liable to | Class 1 Employee and Employer | on | £45,000 | and | Class 1A | on | £300 |.

Task 5.4

The correct answer is:

	✓
True	
False	✓

This is above the statutory maximum of 45p per mile and so Class 1 Employee and Employer would be payable on the excess.

Task 5.5

The correct answer is:

	✓
True	
False	✓

Vouchers are deemed to be cash equivalents and so Class 1 Employee and Employer contributions would be due on the cash amount of the vouchers.

Task 5.6

The correct answer is:

	✓
£nil	
£5,550	
£4,800	✓
£3,665	

Working

£(37,000 – 5,000) × 15% = £4,800. The employment allowance is not available as Freya is the sole employed earner and a director of Wise Ltd.

The answer £nil deducts the employment allowance. The answer £5,550 ignores the employer threshold. The answer £3,665 uses the employee threshold instead of the employer threshold.

Task 5.7

Employers	Class 1A

Employees	None

Employees do not pay national insurance on benefits.

Chapter 6 – Chargeable gains

Task 6.1

For the gain on the disposal of a capital asset to be a chargeable gain there must be a chargeable

disposal

of a chargeable

asset

by a chargeable

person

Task 6.2

The correct answers are:

Item	Chargeable asset ✓	Exempt asset ✓
Car		✓
A plot of land	✓	
Jewellery	✓	
Premium bonds		✓
Government stock ('gilts')		✓

Task 6.3

The correct answer is:

	✓
The gift of an asset	
The sale of part of an asset	
The transfer of an asset on death	✓
The sale of the whole of an asset	

Task 6.4

The correct answer is:

	✓
£42,100	✓
£47,100	
£45,100	
£50,100	

	£
Proceeds of sale	90,100
Less cost	(40,000)
Less enhancement expenditure	(5,000)
Chargeable gain	45,100
Less annual exempt amount	(3,000)
Taxable gain	42,100

The answer £47,100 does not deduct the enhancement expenditure. The answer £45,100 does not deduct the annual exempt amount. The answer £50,100 does not deduct the enhancement expenditure or the annual exempt amount.

Task 6.5

(a) £ 2,602

	£
Chargeable gains	17,400
Less allowable losses	(3,560)
Net chargeable gains	13,840
Less annual exempt amount	(3,000)
Taxable gains	10,840
CGT: 10,840 × 24%	2,602

(b) 31/01/2027

Task 6.6

£ 3,168

	£
Chargeable gains	22,400
Less allowable losses	(5,200)

ANSWERS

	£
Net chargeable gains	17,200
Less annual exempt amount	(3,000)
Taxable gains	14,200

CGT payable

	£
£4,000 × 18%	720
£10,200 × 24%	2,448
	3,168

Task 6.7

£ 3,272

	£
Chargeable gains (£5,400 + £14,500)	19,900
Less allowable losses	(2,000)
Net chargeable gains	17,900
Less annual exempt amount	(3,000)
Taxable gains	14,900

CGT payable

	£
£5,065 (W) × 18%	912
£9,835 × 24%	2,360
	3,272
(W) Unused basic rate band is £37,700 – £32,635 = £5,065	

Task 6.8

£ 4,922

	£
Chargeable gains	25,000
Less annual exempt amount	(3,000)
Taxable gains	22,000
CGT	

	£
£5,965 (W) × 18%	1,074
£16,035 × 24%	3,848
	4,922
(W) Unused basic rate band is £37,700 – £31,735 = £5,965	

Task 6.9

(a) £ 120,000

$$\frac{240,000}{240,000 + 60,000} \times £150,000$$

(b) £ 117,000

	£
Disposal proceeds	240,000
Less disposal costs	(3,000)
Net proceeds	237,000
Less cost	(120,000)
Chargeable gain	117,000

Task 6.10

The correct answer is:

	✓
The full amount will be paid on 31 January 2027	✓
The full amount will be paid on 31 January 2026	
Payments on account will be made on 31 January and 31 July 2026, with the balance being paid on 31 January 2027	
Payments on account will be made on 31 January and 31 July 2025, with the balance being paid on 31 January 2026	

Task 6.11

£ 7,900

	£
Gains	17,100

ANSWERS

	£
Losses	(7,000)
	10,100
Less annual exempt amount	(3,000)
	7,100
Losses b/f	(7,100)
Taxable gains	Nil

Losses c/f £(15,000 – 7,100) = £7,900

Task 6.12

£ 7,000

	£
Proceeds of sale	16,000
Less allowable cost (value at death)	*(9,000)*
Chargeable gain	7,000

Task 6.13

£ 17,000

	£
Proceeds of sale	25,000
Less disposal costs	(2,500)
Net proceeds of sale	22,500
Less allowable cost	
25,000/(25,000 + 50,000) × £(15,000 + 1,500)	(5,500)
Chargeable gain	17,000

Task 6.14

The correct answer is:

	✓
True	✓
False	

If an individual has allowable losses brought forward, these are allocated after the deduction of the annual exemption and can bring the taxable gain down to nil.

Task 6.15

£ 3,000

Tax year	2023/24 £	2024/25 £	2025/26 £
Gains	2,000	4,000	14,000
Losses	(14,000)	(2,000)	(2,000)
Net gain/(loss)	(12,000)	2,000	12,000
Less annual exempt amount	(0)	(2,000)	(3,000)
Less loss b/f	0	0	(9,000)
Chargeable gain	0	0	0
Loss c/f	(12,000)	(12,000)	(3,000)

The loss b/f to 2024/25 was not used as all the gains were covered by the annual exemption. In 2025/26 £9,000 of the loss b/f is used which leaves £3,000 remaining to c/f.

Task 6.16

The correct answer is:

	✓
Beatrice	
Susan	
Simon	
Sarah	✓

Mary is connected to her daughter (Beatrice), her sister-in-law (Susan) and her brother-in-law (Simon). Mary is not connected to her niece (Sarah).

Task 6.17

The correct answer is:

	✓
True	
False	✓

The loss of £(3,000) can only be set against gains on disposals made to the son (ie the same connected person) in the same tax year or future tax years.

Task 6.18

£ 833

ANSWERS

	£
Gross proceeds	6,500
Less costs of sale	(130)
Net proceeds	6,370
Less cost	(1,500)
Chargeable gain	4,870
Gain cannot exceed 5/3 × £(6,500 – 6,000)	833

Task 6.19

£ 1,125

	£
Deemed proceeds	6,000
Less costs of sale	(125)
Net proceeds	5,875
Less cost	(7,000)
Allowable loss	(1,125)

Task 6.20

The correct answer is:

	✓
True	
False	✓

Both the proceeds and the cost are less than £6,000 so the gain is exempt.

Task 6.21

The correct answer is:

	✓
£1,200	
£2,200	
£2,500	✓
£3,700	

	£
Gross proceeds	7,500

	£
Less costs of sale	(300)
Net proceeds	7,200
Less cost	(3,500)
Chargeable gain	3,700
Gain cannot exceed 5/3 × £(7,500 – 6,000)	2,500

The answer £1,200 uses a deemed cost of £6,000. The answer £2,200 uses deemed proceeds of £6,000. The answer £3,700 does not make any chattel adjustments.

Task 6.22

£ (3,500)

	£
Deemed proceeds	6,000
Less costs of sale	(500)
Net proceeds	5,500
Less cost	(9,000)
Allowable loss	(3,500)

ANSWERS

Chapter 7 – Share disposals

Task 7.1

The correct answer is:

	✓
Against 10,000 of the shares purchased on 10 May 2010	
Against 5,000 of the shares purchased on 24 January 2026 and then against 5,000 of the shares purchased on 10 May 2010	
Against 10,000 of the total shareholding of 20,000 shares	
Against the 8,000 shares purchased on 24 January 2026 and then against 2,000 of the shares purchased on 10 May 2010	✓

Task 7.2

£ 9,800

Mr Stevens will match his disposal of 5,000 shares on 10 August 2025 to acquisitions as follows:

(1) 1,000 shares bought on 16 August 2025 (next 30 days, FIFO basis)

(2) 4,000 shares from the share pool (which only consists of the 6,000 shares bought in July 2020)

Disposal of 1,000 shares bought on 16 August 2025

	£
Proceeds of sale £20,000 × 1,000/5,000	4,000
Less cost	(4,200)
Allowable loss	(200)

Disposal of 4,000 shares bought from the share pool (= July 2020 acquisition)

	£
Proceeds of sale £20,000 × 4,000/5,000	16,000
Less cost £9,000 × 4,000/6,000	(6,000)
Chargeable gain	10,000
Net chargeable gain = £10,000 – 200	9,800

Task 7.3

Share pool

	No. of shares	Cost £
10 February 2003	12,000	18,000
20 September 2010 Bonus 1:4 (1/4 × 12,000 = 3,000 shares)	3,000	0
	15,000	18,000
15 March 2026 Disposal (£18,000 × 2,000/15,000 = £2,400)	(2,000)	(2,400)
	13,000	15,600

Gain on sale

	£
Proceeds	8,000
Less cost	(2,400)
Gain	5,600

Task 7.4

Mark will match his disposal of 10,000 shares on 4 November 2025 as follows:

(1) 2,000 shares bought on 10 November 2025

(2) 8,000 shares from share pool

	£
Disposal of 2,000 shares bought on 10 November 2025:	
Proceeds 2,000/10,000 × £60,000	12,000
Less cost	(11,500)
Chargeable gain	500
Disposal of 8,000 shares from share pool:	
Proceeds 8,000/10,000 × £60,000	48,000
Less cost (W)	(12,200)
Chargeable gain	35,800
Total chargeable gain (£500 + £35,800)	36,300

Share pool working	No. of shares	Cost £
9 December 2003	12,000	4,400
12 October 2007 Rights 1:3 × £5	4,000	20,000

ANSWERS

Share pool working	No. of shares	Cost £
(1/3 × 12,000 = 4,000 shares × £5 = £20,000)		
	16,000	24,400
4 November 2025 Disposal	(8,000)	(12,200)
(£24,400 × 8,000/16,000 = £12,200)		
	8,000	12,200

Task 7.5

	£
Disposal proceeds	3,675,000
Less cost (W)	(537,600)
Chargeable gain	3,137,400

Working

Share pool

	Number	Cost £
Purchase June 2008	500,000	960,000
Bonus issue December 2013		
500,000 × 3/2	750,000	0
Disposal September 2025	1,250,000	960,000
960,000 × 700,000/1,250,000	(700,000)	(537,600)
Balance carried forward	550,000	422,400

Chapter 8 – Private residence relief

Task 8.1

The correct answer is:

	✓
16.5/25	✓
10.75/25	
15.75/25	
8.5/25	

	Chargeable	Exempt
Actual occupation		8.75
Employment abroad (actual occupation before and after period of absence) – any period		5
Actual occupation		2
Absence (not followed by period of actual occupation)	8.5	
Last nine months of ownership		0.75
Totals	8.5	16.5

The answer 10.75/25 is periods of actual occupation only. The answer 15.75/25 ignores the last nine months deemed residence. The answer 8.5/25 is the chargeable fraction.

Task 8.2

The correct answer is:

	✓
True	✓
False	

The period when the property was unoccupied will be covered by the last nine months deemed occupation rule.

Task 8.3

	£
Proceeds	180,000
Less cost	(50,000)
Gain before private residence exemption	130,000
Less private residence exemption (9.25/(9.25 + 10.75) × 130,000)	(60,125)
Chargeable gain	69,875

ANSWERS

Working

	Exempt years	Chargeable years
1.8.05 – 31.7.08 (actual occupation)	3	
1.8.08 – 31.7.12 (up to 4 years due to place of work not employed abroad)	4	
1.8.12 – 31.7.13 (covered by up to 3 years any reason)	1	
1.8.13 – 31.1.14 (actual occupation)	0.5	
1.2.14 – 20.10.24 (not followed by actual occupation)		10.75
1.11.24 – 31.7.25 (last nine months)	0.75	
Totals	9.25	10.75

Task 8.4

The correct answer is:

	✓
13.75/14.5	✓
13.5/14.5	
10.5/14.5	
10.75/14.5	

	Exempt years	Chargeable years	Total years
Actual occupation	3		3
Deemed occupation – any time employed overseas	5		5
Actual occupation	2		2
Deemed occupation – up to 3 years any reason	3		3
Unoccupied		0.75	0.75
Last nine months of ownership	0.75		0.75
Totals	13.75	0.75	14.5

The answer 13.5/14.5 ignores the final nine months of deemed ownership. The answer 10.5/14.5 ignores deemed occupation for three years for any reason and the final nine months. The answer 10.75/14.5 ignores the deemed occupation for three years for any reason eg forgets Jose returned to the house for the final six months.

Task 8.5

The correct answer is:

	✓
True	
False	✓

Periods of time working abroad are only covered by the deemed occupation rules if the owner lives in the property before and after the absence.

ANSWERS

Chapter 9 – Inheritance tax

Task 9.1

The correct answers are:

	PET ✓	Exempt ✓
Gift of £100 cash to niece **Explanation:** Small gift.		✓
Gift of property which is rented out worth £100,000 to daughter	✓	
Gift of £5,000 to son on the occasion of his marriage		✓
Gift of £25,000 to a friend	✓	
Gift of classic car to spouse **Explanation:** Transfers between spouses/civil partners are exempt.		✓

Task 9.2

£ 550,000

Norman's nil band at death was £325,000 with £100,000 being used on the transfer to his cousin. The remaining £225,000 is added to the nil band of Maureen of £325,000 making a total nil band of £550,000 available to Maureen on her death.

Task 9.3

The correct answers are:

	Deductible ✓	Not deductible ✓
Grocery bill **Explanation:** Deductible as incurred for consideration	✓	
HM Revenue & Customs – income tax to death **Explanation:** Deductible as imposed by law	✓	
Mortgage on home **Explanation:** Deductible, will be set against value of house primarily	✓	
Illegal gambling debt **Explanation:** Not deductible as not legally enforceable		✓

Task 9.4

The correct answer is:

	✓
True	
False	✓

A PET is only subject to Inheritance Tax on the death of the donor if the death occurs within seven years of the gift

Task 9.5

The correct answer is:

	✓
True	
False	✓

The £5,000 exemption only applies to gifts on marriage from parent to child.

Task 9.6

The correct answer is:

Lifetime tax	Death tax	✓
31 January 2026	30 June 2026	
30 April 2026	30 June 2026	✓
31 January 2026	30 April 2026	
30 April 2026	30 April 2026	

Lifetime tax 30 April 2026, death tax 30 June 2026

For chargeable lifetime transfers the due date is the later of 30 April just after the end of the tax year of the transfer and six months after the end of the month of the transfer. The due date for the tax arising on death is six months from the end of the month of death.

Task 9.7

The correct answer is:

	✓
0%	
20%	
25%	✓
40%	

The gross chargeable transfer in August 2024 will have used up the nil rate band. As Bernard, the donor, is paying the IHT the lifetime rate is 25%. If the donee paid the tax the lifetime rate would be 20%. 40% is the death tax rate.

Task 9.8

60 %

Kalila survived 5 but not 6 years from the date of the gift. Therefore, the taper relief percentage is 60%.

Task 9.9

£ 2,750

Working

	£
Before transfer: 500 shares at £10	5,000
After transfer: 300 shares at £7.50	2,250
Transfer of value	2,750

Task 9.10

The correct answer is:

	✓
£6,000	
£4,000	✓
£3,000	
£1,000	

Working

	£
PET September 2025	2,000
Less AE cy	(2,000)
CLT February 2026	6,000
Less AE cy remaining (£3,000 – £2,000)	(1,000)
Less AE bf	(3,000)

Therefore, the correct answer is £1,000 + £3,000 = £4,000

The answer £6,000 does not offset the annual exemption in chronological order. The answer £3,000 does not offset in chronological order and ignores the brought forward annual exemption. The answer £1,000 ignores the brought forward annual exemption.

Chapter 10 – The tax and ethical framework

Task 10.1

06/04/2025

until:

05/04/2026

Task 10.2

The correct answer is:

	✓
True	✓
False	

Task 10.3

The correct answer is:

	✓
Parliament	
His Majesty's Revenue & Customs (HMRC)	✓
National Crime Agency (NCA)	
HM Customs & Excise	

Task 10.4

The correct answer is:

	✓
HMRC	
Your firm's Money Laundering Reporting Officer	✓
National Crime Agency	
Tax Tribunal	

Task 10.5

Please be assured that an ethical guideline of confidentiality applies in your dealings with our firm.

This guideline means that your personal information will remain confidential, unless you give us authority to disclose information to third parties such as members of your family.

Task 10.6

The correct answers are:

	✓
If the client is unwell and unable to respond to HMRC	
If money laundering is suspected	✓
Where it would be illegal not to disclose the information	✓
If the information is requested from a 'connected person'	

Task 10.7

I	Integrity
O	Objectivity
Pc and dc	Professional competence and due care
C	Confidentiality
Pb	Professional behaviour

Task 10.8

The correct answer is:

	✓
HMRC	
Another firm's Money Laundering Reporting Officer	
National Crime Agency	✓
Tax Tribunal	

Task 10.9

The correct answer is:

	✓
True	
False	✓

A non-UK resident individual is only liable to pay income tax on their UK income.

Task 10.10

You should inform the client that this represents theft and they should tell HMRC of their mistake immediately.

If they refuse to tell HMRC then you will need to warn them of the consequences of not informing HMRC of their mistake. If HMRC do discover this error, then there would be interest and penalties (criminal and civil) due as well as the expectation that the initial amount of the refund would need to be repaid.

If they still refuse, then you should cease to act for the client and inform HMRC that you have ceased to act for them. You cannot tell HMRC why you are ceasing to act for the client as this would be a breach of confidentiality.

You have a professional responsibility to neither break the law nor assist others to do so.

Ensure all correspondence is in writing and saved in the file.

Task 10.11

The correct answer is:

	✓
True	
False	✓

Tax avoidance is the use of tax legislation in a way that was not intended to reduce tax liabilities. It is legal but can be considered unethical.

Tax evasion is illegal.

AAT Practice Assessment

Personal Tax FA 2025

You are advised to attempt practice assessments online from the AAT website. This will ensure you are prepared for how the assessment will be presented on the AAT's system when you attempt the real assessment. Please access the assessment using the address below:

https://www.aat.org.uk/training/study-support/search

The AAT may call the assessments on their website, under study support resources, either a 'practice assessment' or 'sample assessment'.

BPP Practice Assessment 1

Personal Tax FA 2025

Time allowed: 2 hours 30 minutes

Personal Tax FA 2025

BPP Practice Assessment 1

Assessment information

You have **2 1/2 hours** to complete this sample assessment.

- This assessment contains **10 tasks** and you should attempt to complete every task.
- Each task is independent. You will not need to refer to your answers in previous tasks.
- The total number of marks for this assessment is 100.
- Read every task carefully to make sure you understand what is required.
- Where the date is relevant, it is given in the task data.
- Both minus signs or brackets can be used to indicate negative numbers **unless** task instructions say otherwise.
- You must use a full stop to indicate a decimal point. For example, write 100.57 NOT 100,57 or 100 57.
- You may use a comma to indicate a number in the thousands, but you don't have to. For example, 10000 and 10,000 are both acceptable.
- If your answer requires rounding, apply normal mathematical rules **unless** the task instructions say otherwise

In the live assessment you will have access to the tax tables and reference material which have been reproduced at the back of this Question Bank. Please use them while completing this practice assessment so that you are familiar with their content.

Task 1 (10 marks)

You work for a firm of accountants. A few weeks ago, you prepared a tax return for Sharon.

Sharon has a home in London and a home in Spain that she rents out at certain times of year and when it is not rented out, she stays in the property. Sharon spent 189 days in the UK during the 2025/26 tax year.

She has now told you that she has some property income from the second home in Spain that was not included in the return but that she does not intend to tell HM Revenue & Customs (HMRC) about the income as it does not arise in the UK.

Required

(a) Summarise Sharon's residency status and how she will be taxed in the UK for 2025/26. You should also state whether the non-disclosure of the Spanish property income is tax avoidance or tax evasion.

(3 marks)

Sharon's husband Derek is also a client of your firm. Derek has informed you that he forgot to tell you about some bank interest that he received which should have been included in his last tax return. He does not want to inform HMRC as the return has already been submitted and he doesn't want to amend it.

Required

(b) Explain what steps you should take regarding this information.

(7 marks)

Task 2 (14 marks)

Shane is provided with a company car for business and private use throughout 2025/26. The car had a list price of £16,700, although the company paid £15,000 for the car after a dealer discount. It has CO_2 emissions of 93g/km. The company pays for all running costs, including all fuel. Shane does not make any contribution for his private use of the car.

Required

(a) Complete the following sentences:

(1) The cost of the car in the taxable benefit computation is:

£ [ ]

(2) The percentage used in the taxable benefit computation is:

[ ] %

(3) The taxable benefit in respect of the provision of fuel for private use is:

[ ]

(4 marks)

(b) Complete the following table by inserting the scale charge for 2025/26 for each of the cars shown below.

	CO_2 emissions	Scale charge %
Car 1	131	%
Car 2	172	%

(2 marks)

Josie is a basic rate taxpayer and receives the following benefits as the result of her employment.

Required

(c) In each case enter the taxable benefit arising in 2025/26. If the benefit is exempt, enter 0.

(5 marks)

(i) A mobile telephone for private and business use throughout the year. The purchase of the phone and the calls from it cost her employer a total of £350 for 2025/26.

£ [ ]

(ii) Payment of £50 for incidental overnight expenses whilst staying away in the UK for five nights.

£ [ ]

(iii) Leisure club membership for Josie costing her employer £5,000 using a corporate discount scheme. If a member of the public had taken this membership it would have cost £6,500.

£ [ ]

(iv) Use of a house near her work that enables her to start work at 7.00am every morning. The house has an annual value of £5,900 and cost her employer £227,000 4 years ago.

£ [ ]

(d) Identify whether the following statements are true or false:

Item	True ✓	False ✓
An interest-free loan of £8,000 is an exempt benefit (only loan provided)		
Shana claims expenses of costs of home working of £7 per week (no evidence presented to employer). This is an exempt benefit.		

Item	True ✓	False ✓
Eric is an employee of Border Ltd. He receives a bonus of £5,000 on 30 April 2026 in relation to the accounting year ended 31 March 2026. He will be taxed on the bonus in 2025/26.		

(3 marks)

Task 3 (10 marks)

During 2025/26, Eva received a dividend from a UK company of £465. Her other taxable income totalled £40,000.

Required

(a) How much tax is payable on the dividends?

£ [ ]

(1 mark)

During 2025/26 Geraint received government stock ('gilt') interest of £100, building society interest of £600 and interest on an ISA account of £300. Geraint also has taxable income from his employment of £60,000

Required

(b) Complete the following sentences.

(1) Geraint's taxable savings income is

£ [ ]

(2) The tax payable on Geraint's savings income is

£ [ ]

(3 marks)

Emily lets a furnished house from 1 June 2025. Rent of £600 per month is due in advance, payable on the 1st of the month.

During 2025/26, Emily spent £190 on advertising for tenants, £460 on water rates, £800 on redecoration, and £368 on cleaning. Emily also installed a new central heating system at a cost of £1,200. Previously, the house did not have central heating. Emily replaced some furniture at a cost of £1,244 during 2025/26.

Emily uses the accruals basis to calculate her property profits.

Required

(c) Calculate the property income taxable on Emily for 2025/26 using the proforma layout provided. Fill in all the unshaded boxes. If any item is not an allowable expense, enter 0. Both brackets and minus signs can be used to show negative numbers.

	£
Rent accrued	
Expenses:	
Advertising	
Water rates	

	£
Redecoration	
Cleaning	
Central heating system	
Furniture cost	
Property income	

(4 marks)

(d) Identify whether the following statements are true or false

	True ✓	False ✓
Oliver has property income of £2,200 and allowable expenses of £600. He should elect to use the property allowance.		
Gita buys a double bed for her rental property at a cost of £800 to replace a single bed. A new single bed would have cost £500. The allowable expense is £800.		

(2 marks)

Task 4 (14 marks)

During 2025/26 Elaine earned the following income:

	£
Employment income (PAYE paid of £36,432)	125,000
Bank interest	5,000
Individual savings account interest	2,000
Income from property	3,000
Dividends	4,000

Elaine has losses from property brought forward of £4,000. During the year, Elaine contributed 8% of her salary into her employer's pension scheme. Her employer paid an additional 3%. Elaine also made a donation to charity of £4,800 in the year.

Required

Calculate her total income tax payable to the nearest pound for 2025/26, entering your answer and workings in the blank table given below.

(14 marks)

Task 5 (6 marks)

Tom has employment income of £75,000 in 2025/26. He is provided with a company car and private fuel throughout the year. The taxable benefit arising from these benefits totals £4,500.

Required

(a) Complete the following sentences by typing your answer, in whole pounds, in the boxes provided. Ignore the employment allowance.

(4 marks)

(i) The total Class 1 employee's national insurance contributions payable by Tom in 2025/26 are:

£ [ ]

(ii) The total Class 1 employer's national insurance contributions payable by Tom's employer in 2025/26 are:

£ [ ]

(iii) The total Class 1A national insurance contributions payable by Tom's employer in 2025/26 are:

£ [ ]

(b) Identify whether the following statements are true or false

Statement	True ✓	False ✓
All employers are entitled to the employment allowance, including companies where the director is the only employee.		
Jennifer earns a salary of £9,500 and receives benefits totalling £5,000. She will not have to pay any class 1 national insurance contributions.		

(2 marks)

Task 6 (8 marks)

Complete the following sentences. Assume rates and allowances remain the same as 2025/26.

Tia has use of a car which had a list price of £18,000 and an annual taxable benefit of £4,140.

Tia is considering upgrading to a new electric car with the same list price, CO_2 emissions of 49g/km, and an electric mileage range of 89 miles. This would reduce her annual taxable benefit by:

Required

(a) £ [ ]

(2 marks)

Fiona has annual income of £114,000.

Fiona is considering making pension contributions to a personal pension scheme and would like to preserve her personal allowance. She would need to make a pension contribution of:

Required

(b) £ [ ]

(2 marks)

Bert is a higher rate taxpayer. During 2025/26 he has made chargeable gains of £15,000. He is considering disposing of shares either on 31 March 2026 or 30 April 2026 with an expected chargeable gain of £20,000.

If he delays the disposal until 30 April 2026, he will save capital gains tax of:

Required

(c) £ [ ]

(2 marks)

Malik has employment income of £55,000 and interest from a building society account of £5,000.

Malik is considering switching his investment to an ISA with the same rate of interest. This would save him income tax of:

Required

(d) £ [ ]

(2 marks)

Task 7 (10 marks)

(a) For each of the following assets, tick the relevant column to indicate whether they are chargeable or exempt assets for capital gains tax:

Asset	Chargeable ✓	Exempt ✓
Car used solely for business purposes		
Holiday cottage		
Vintage car worth £40,000		
Shares held in an individual savings account		

(4 marks)

Rodney purchased an antique chair for £1,450. On 10 October 2025 he sold the chair at auction for £6,300 (which was net of the auctioneer's 10% commission).

Required

(b) The chargeable gain on sale is:

£ [ ]

(2 marks)

Andrew bought six acres of land for £405,000. He sold two acres of the land at auction for £360,000. His disposal costs were £6,000. The market value of the four remaining acres at the date of sale was £540,000.

Required

(c) Complete the following sentences.

(4 marks)

(i) The cost of the land sold is:

£ [ ]

(ii) **The chargeable gain on sale is:**

£ [ ]

Task 8 (8 marks)

In August 2012 Wayne acquired 4,000 shares in Main plc at a cost of £10,000. In September 2014, there was a one for one bonus issue when the shares were worth £8 each. Wayne sold 3,000 shares in July 2015 for £15,000 and purchased 3,000 back again in October 2015 for £12,000.

Wayne sold half of his shareholding in June 2025 for £21,000.

Required

Clearly showing the balance of shares and their value to carry forward, calculate the gain made on the sale of the shares in 2025/26. All workings must be shown in your calculations.

(8 marks)

Task 9 (10 marks)

(a) **For each of the following statements, tick if they are True or False.**

	True ✓	False ✓
Any CGT annual exempt amount that is unused in one tax year can be carried forward to be used in the following tax year only.		

	True ✓	False ✓
Capital losses in a tax year must be offset against capital gains in that year, even if it means losing all, or some of the annual exempt amount.		
Assets transferred between civil partners will not result in a chargeable gain or allowable loss.		

(3 marks)

Charlotte bought a house on 1 February 2013 for £95,000 and sold it for £263,000 on 1 October 2025. During the period of ownership, the following occurred:

01.02.13 to 31.10.15	Charlotte lived in the property
01.11.15 to 31.03.24	Charlotte worked elsewhere in the UK
01.04.24 to 30.09.25	Charlotte lived in the property until she sold it

Required

(b) Input the correct answers in the boxes provided to complete the sentences. Where applicable, round your answer to the nearest whole number.

The total period of ownership of the property is [ ] months.

The period of Charlotte's actual and deemed residence is [ ] months.

The chargeable gain on the sale of the house is £ [ ]

(3 marks)

Ella purchased an antique necklace for £12,000. She sold it on 1 September 2025 for £63,000. Ella has no other chargeable assets. Her taxable income for 2025/26 was £34,700.

Required

(c) Complete the following sentences.

(2 marks)

(i) Ella's CGT payable on the antique necklace for 2025/26 is:

£ [ ]

(ii) This is payable by (XX/XX/XXXX):

[ ]

Brad has capital gains in 2025/26 of £30,000 and capital losses of £15,600. He also has a loss brought forward from 2024/25 of £15,000.

Required

(d) Complete the following sentences.

(2 marks)

(i) The amount chargeable, if any, to capital gains tax is:

£ [ ]

(ii) The amount of losses, if any, carried forward to 2026/27 is

£ [ ]

Task 10 (10 marks)

(a) **For each of the following statements, tick if they are true or false.**

	True ✓	False ✓
A CLT is only chargeable on death of the donor.		
Cars are exempt from IHT.		
The annual exemption for the current year is used before any unused annual exemption brought forward from the prior year.		
Hilda makes a gift to her granddaughter of £200 in August 2025 and an additional £300 in February 2026. Only the second gift would be a PET.		
An additional rate taxpayer pays IHT at 45%.		

(5 marks)

(b) **Complete the following statements.**

(3 marks)

Joshi makes the following lifetime transfers prior to her death in December 2025:

(1) PET of £45,000 in January 2017

(2) CLT of £30,000 in April 2018

(3) CLT of £25,000 in June 2023

Required

(i) **The transfers which are taken into account for the nil rate band available in calculating the death tax on the June 2023 CLT are:**

	✓
(1) only	
(2) only	
(1) and (2)	
Neither	

Inga made a lifetime transfer in February 2026 of £4,500. She did not make any transfers in 2024/25.

Required

(ii) **The amount of annual exemption which may be carried forward to 2026/27 is:**

	✓
£3,000	
£0	
£1,500	
£4,500	

Hugo made a PET in June 2020. He died in July 2025.

Required

(iii) The taper relief available on the transfer is:

	✓
20%	
40%	
60%	
80%	

Andy and Hilda had been married for many years when Andy died in June 2015. 60% of Andy's nil rate band was unused on his death. The nil rate band at Andy's death was £325,000. Hilda died in December 2025. Her only lifetime transfers of value were cash gifts of £6,000 to her nephew in January 2025 and £10,000 to her niece in March 2025. Hilda did not own any property on her death.

Required

(c) Complete the following sentences

(2 marks)

(i) The unused nil rate band transferred from Andy to Hilda is:

£ [ ]

(ii) The total nil rate band available for use against Hilda's estate is:

£ [ ]

BPP Practice Assessment 1

Personal Tax FA 2025

Answers

Task 1

(a) As Sharon has been in the UK for 189 days during the 2025/26 tax year, she meets the first condition of the automatically UK resident test and will therefore be UK resident.

She will be subject to tax in the UK on her worldwide income and gains on an arising basis. Sharon must therefore inform HMRC about her Spanish property income.

If Sharon does not disclose the Spanish property income to HMRC, this will be classed as tax evasion and failing to declare income is illegal.

(b) You should inform Derek of the implications of not reporting this income to HMRC and that it could be viewed as tax evasion which is punishable by fines/imprisonment.

If he refuses to inform HMRC of this income then you should let him know, in writing, that it is not possible for your firm to continue to act for him.

You should then inform HMRC that your firm is no longer acting for Derek but you should not give details of why you are ceasing to act as this would be a breach of confidentiality.

You should then make a report to your firm's Money Laundering Reporting Officer of Derek's refusal to disclose the omission to HMRC and the facts surrounding it.

Task 2

(a) (1) The cost of the car in the taxable benefit computation is:

£ 16,700

(2) The percentage used in the taxable benefit computation is:

24 %

(3) The taxable benefit in respect of the provision of fuel for private use is:

6,768

The cost of the car is the list price, discounts are ignored.

The percentage is calculated: 17% + (90 – 55)/5%

The taxable benefit for fuel is: £28,200 × 24%

(b)

	CO_2 emissions	Scale charge %
Car 1	131	32%
Car 2	172	37%

17% + (130 – 55)/5 = 32%

17% + (170 – 55)/5 = 40% (max 37%)

(c) **(i)** £ 0

(ii) £ 50

If paid over £5 per night for stays in the UK then the whole amount is taxable.

(iii) £ 5,000

(iv) £ 11,600

£5,900 + ((£227,000 – 75,000) × 3.75%))

(d) The correct answers are:

Item	True ✓	False ✓
An interest-free loan of £8,000 is an exempt benefit (only loan provided) **Explanation:** (£10,000 or less)	✓	
Shana claims expenses of costs of home working of £7 per week (no evidence presented to employer). This is an exempt benefit. **Explanation:** (evidence needed if more than £6 per week)		✓
Eric is an employee of Border Ltd. He receives a bonus of £5,000 on 30 April 2026 in relation to the accounting year ended 31 March 2026. He will be taxed on the bonus in 2025/26. **Explanation:** (as employee earlier of date received and entitlement)		✓

Task 3

(a) £ 0

The dividend allowance of £500 is available to all taxpayers.

(b) (1) Geraint's taxable savings income is

£ 700

(2) The tax payable on Geraint's savings income is

£ 80

Gilts and building society interests are taxable as interest income. ISA interest is exempt.

Geraint is a higher rate taxpayer so is entitled to a savings allowance of £500. The remainder is taxed at 40%. 40% × (£700 – £500)

(c)

	£
Rent accrued £600 × 10 (accruals basis)	6,000
Expenses:	
Advertising	(190)
Water rates	(460)
Redecoration	(800)
Cleaning	(368)
Central heating system (capital)	(0)
Furniture cost	(1,244)
Property income	2,938

(d) The correct answers are:

	True ✓	False ✓
Oliver has property income of £2,200 and allowable expenses of £600. He should elect to use the property allowance. **Explanation:** (£1,200 taxable property income compared to £1,600)	✓	
Gita buys a double bed for her rental property at a cost of £800 to replace a single bed. A new single bed would have cost £500. The allowable expense is £800. **Explanation:** (equivalent replacement only)		✓

Task 4

	Non-savings £	Interest £	Dividends £
Employment Income	125,000		
Employee pension contribution (8% × £125,000)	(10,000)		
Employer pension contribution (exempt benefit)	0		
Property income	3,000		
Property loss (only against property income)	(3,000)		
Bank interest		5,000	
ISA interest (exempt)		0	
Dividends			4,000
Net income	115,000	5,000	4,000
Personal allowance (W1)	(3,570)		
Taxable income	111,430	5,000	4,000
£43,700 (W2) × 20%	8,740		
£67,730 (£111,430 – £43,700) × 40%	27,092		
£500 × 0%	0		
£4,500 × 40%	1,800		
£500 × 0%	0		
£3,500 × 33.75%	1,181		
Income tax liability	38,813		
PAYE	(36,432)		

	Non-savings £	Interest £	Dividends £
Income tax payable	2,381		
Working 1 - personal allowance			
Net income (£115,000 + £5,000 + £4,000)	124,000		
Gift aid payment (100/80 × £4,800)	(6,000)		
Adjusted net income	118,000		
Personal allowance	12,570		
Abatement (1/2 × (£118,000 – £100,000)	(9,000)		
	3,570		
Working 2 - basic rate band extension due to gift aid donation			
37,700 + (100/80 × £4,800)	£43,700		

Task 5

(a) **(i)** £ 3,511

(£50,270 – £12,570) × 8% = £3,016

(£75,000 – £50,270) × 2% = £495

(ii) £ 10,500

(£75,000 – £5,000) × 15% = £10,500

(iii) £ 675

£4,500 × 15% = £675

(b) The correct answers are:

Statement	True ✓	False ✓
All employers are entitled to the employment allowance, including companies where the director is the only employee. **Explanation:** (Companies where the director is the only employee are excluded from the employment allowance)		✓
Jennifer earns a salary of £9,500 and receives benefits totalling £5,000. She will not have to pay any class 1 national insurance contributions. **Explanation:** (< threshold for class 1 employee. Class 1 employer and class 1A are payable by the employer)	✓	

Task 6

(a) £ 3,060

Taxable benefit percentage of the current car = £4,140/£18,000 = 23%

The new car has a taxable benefit percentage of 6% for an electric car with a mileage of 70-129 and CO_2 emissions below 50g/km

Upgrading to a new car reduces benefit percentage by 17% to 6%

Reduction in taxable benefit = £4,140 – (6% × £18,000) or 17% of £18,000

(b) £ 11,200

Adjusted net income currently = £114,000

Gross pension contribution required = £14,000

Net pension contribution required = 80/100 × £14,000 = £11,200

(c) £ 720

£3,000 × 24%

If he made the disposal on 31 March 2026 the total gain would be taxed at 24% as he has already made gains in excess of his annual exempt amount. If the disposal is delayed until 30 April 2026, another annual exempt amount will be available to reduce the gain.

(d) £ 1,800

Malik is a higher rate taxpayer as his taxable employment income is greater than the basic rate threshold. Tax on his interest (which would be saved if he switched to an ISA) is therefore £1,800 (£500 × 0% + £4,500 × 40%).

Task 7

(a) The correct answers are:

Asset	Chargeable ✓	Exempt ✓
Car used solely for business purposes		✓
Holiday cottage	✓	
Vintage car worth £40,000		✓
Shares held in an individual savings account		✓

(b) £ 1,667

	£
Disposal proceeds £6,300 × 100/90	7,000
Less disposal costs £7,000 × 10%	(700)
Net proceeds	6,300
Less cost	(1,450)

ANSWERS

	£
Gain	4,850
Cannot exceed 5/3 × £(7,000 – 6,000)	1,667

(c) **(i)** £ 162,000

$$\frac{360{,}000}{360{,}000 + 540{,}000} \times £405{,}000$$

(ii) £ 192,000

	£
Disposal proceeds	360,000
Less disposal costs	(6,000)
Net proceeds	354,000
Less cost	(162,000)
Chargeable gain	192,000

Task 8

	£
Proceeds of sale	21,000
Less cost	(9,125)
Gain	11,875

	No. of shares	Cost £
August 2012 Acquisition	4,000	10,000
September 2014 Bonus 1 for 1	4,000	nil
	8,000	10,000
July 2015 Disposal (3,000/8,000 × £10,000)	(3,000)	(3,750)
	5,000	6,250
October 2015 Acquisition	3,000	12,000
	8,000	18,250
June 2025 Disposal (4,000/8,000 × £18,250)	(4,000)	(9,125)
c/f	4,000	9,125

Task 9

(a) The correct answers are:

	True ✓	False ✓
Any CGT annual exempt amount that is unused in one tax year can be carried forward to be used in the following tax year only.		✓
Capital losses in a tax year must be offset against capital gains in that year, even if it means losing all, or some of the annual exempt amount.	✓	
Assets transferred between civil partners will not result in a chargeable gain or allowable loss.	✓	

Any unused annual exempt amount is lost.

Only capital losses brought forward can be restricted to ensure the annual exempt amount isn't lost.

Transfers between spouses/civil partners are deemed to take place on a no gain/no loss basis with the acquirer taking on the base cost of the disposer.

(b) The total period of ownership of the property is 152 months.

The period of Charlotte's actual and deemed residence is 135 months.

The chargeable gain on the sale of the house is £ 18,789

01.02.13 to 31.10.15	33 months actual occupation
01.11.15 to 31.03.24	48 months – deemed occupation – working elsewhere in UK – preceded and followed by actual occupation
	36 months – deemed occupation – any reason – preceded and followed by actual occupation
	17 months non-occupation
01.04.24 to 30.09.25	18 months – actual occupation (last nine months always deemed occupation anyway)

	£
Disposal proceeds	263,000
Less cost	(95,000)
	168,000
Private residence relief £168,000 × 135/152	(149,211)
Chargeable gain	18,789

(c) **(i)** £ 11,340

(ii) 31/01/2027

ANSWERS

	£
Disposal proceeds	63,000
Less cost	(12,000)
Gain	51,000
Less annual exempt amount	(3,000)
Taxable gain	48,000
CGT	
On £3,000 × 18% (unused basic rate band £37,700 – £34,700)	540
On £45,000 × 24%	10,800
CGT liability	11,340

(d) **(i)** £ 0

£30,000 – £15,600 (current year loss) – £3,000 (AEA) – £11,400 (brought forward loss)

(ii) £ 3,600

£15,000 – £11,400

Task 10

(a) The correct answers are:

	True ✓	False ✓
A CLT is only chargeable on death of the donor. **Explanation:** (chargeable in lifetime)		✓
Cars are exempt from IHT. **Explanation:** (only exempt from CGT)		✓
The annual exemption for the current year is used before any unused annual exemption brought forward from the prior year.	✓	
Hilda makes a gift to her granddaughter of £200 in August 2025 and an additional £300 in February 2026. Only the second gift would be a PET. **Explanation:** (If total gifts to one recipient >£250 all chargeable)		✓
An additional rate taxpayer pays IHT at 45%. **Explanation:** (income tax rate)		✓

(b) (i) The correct answer is:

	✓
(1) only	
(2) only	✓
(1) and (2)	
Neither	

Although (1) is less than seven years before June 2023, it is more than seven years prior to death so becomes exempt.

(2) is less than seven years before June 2023 and, as it was a CLT, is still a chargeable transfer even though it occurred more than seven years prior to death.

(ii) The correct answer is:

	✓
£3,000	
£0	✓
£1,500	
£4,500	

The current year annual exempt is used before the annual exemption brought forward.

(iii) The correct answer is:

	✓
20%	
40%	
60%	✓
80%	

Hugo survived five but not six years, so the amount of taper relief is 60%

(c) (i) £ 195,000

(ii) £ 510,000

	£
Andy's unused nil band: (60% × £325,000)	195,000
Hilda's nil band at death (325,000 – 10,000)	315,000
Total nil band available to Hilda	510,000

The cash gift to Hilda's nephew (a PET) is covered by her annual exemptions (2 × £3,000) so does not use up any of the nil rate band.

BPP Practice Assessment 2

Personal Tax FA 2025

Time allowed: 2 hours 30 minutes

Personal Tax FA 2025

BPP Practice Assessment 2

Assessment information

You have **2 1/2 hours** to complete this sample assessment.

- This assessment contains **10 tasks** and you should attempt to complete every task.
- Each task is independent. You will not need to refer to your answers in previous tasks.
- The total number of marks for this assessment is 100.
- Read every task carefully to make sure you understand what is required.
- Where the date is relevant, it is given in the task data.
- Both minus signs or brackets can be used to indicate negative numbers **unless** task instructions say otherwise.
- You must use a full stop to indicate a decimal point. For example, write 100.57 NOT 100,57 or 100 57.
- You may use a comma to indicate a number in the thousands, but you don't have to. For example, 10000 and 10,000 are both acceptable.
- If your answer requires rounding, apply normal mathematical rules **unless** the task instructions say otherwise

In the live assessment you will have access to the tax tables and reference material which have been reproduced at the back of this Question Bank. Please use them while completing this practice assessment so that you are familiar with their content.

Task 1 (10 marks)

You work for a small firm of Chartered Accountants. A friend of yours has been looking for a property to rent for a while and has been telling you about this person they met a few days ago. It turns out that this person is one of your clients (you do not disclose this to your friend), and your friend tells you about the 20 different properties that this person has. You know that this client has one rental property and that is all that has been disclosed on their tax return.

Required

(a) **Using the AAT guidelines 'Professional Conduct in Relation to Taxation', explain what steps you should take regarding this information.**

(8 marks)

(b) **Which fundamental principle does the following describe?**

To maintain professional knowledge and skill at the level required to ensure that a client or employer receives competent professional service based on current developments in practice, legislation and techniques and acts diligently and in accordance with applicable technical and professional standards.

▼

Picklist

- Confidentiality
- Integrity
- Objectivity
- Professional behaviour
- Professional competence and due care

(1 mark)

(c) **Discussing client affairs with your friend in the pub who is thinking of investing in the client's company would be a breach of which fundamental principle?**

▼

Picklist

- Confidentiality
- Integrity
- Objectivity
- Professional behaviour
- Professional competence and due care

(1 mark)

Task 2 (14 marks)

Steel Ltd provided Susan with a company car from 1 September 2025 for private and business use. The car cost £13,800 and has CO_2 emissions of 93g/km. Susan used the car for 7 months of 2025/26. Steel Ltd pays for all the running costs which amount to £950 and for private fuel which cost £4,000.

Required

(a) Complete the following sentences

(4 marks)

(i) The scale charge percentage for the car is:

[ ] %

(ii) The taxable benefit for the car is:

£ [ ]

(iii) If Susan had contributed £6,000 to the cost of the car, the taxable benefit would be:

£ [ ]

(iv) The fuel benefit for the car is:

£ [ ]

(b) Complete the following sentences

Matthew is provided with a company van for the whole of 2025/26. The only private use of the van is the commute from home to work.

The taxable benefit for use of the van is:

£ [ ]

Luke is provided with a company van on 6 April 2025 which he uses for both personal and business purposes. The company pays for all of the fuel. He was made redundant on 6 October 2025, and he returned the van to the company on that date.

The taxable benefit for use of the van and private fuel is:

£ [ ]

(2 marks)

(c) For each of the following benefits provided to Emily by her employer Bloom Ltd, calculate the amount of the taxable benefit for 2025/26. If a benefit is exempt, enter 0.

(2 marks)

(i) Bloom Ltd gave Emily a loan on 1 August 2025 of £6,000 to pay for home improvements. Emily pays the company 1% interest on the loan but has not repaid any of the loan itself.

The taxable benefit for 2025/26 is:

£ [ ]

(ii) On 1 May 2025 Bloom Ltd provided her with a mobile telephone costing £150 for private and business use.

The taxable benefit for 2025/26 is:

£ [ ]

Bella's employer provided her with a house on 1 April 2025, when it was valued at £125,000. The employer had bought the house for £80,000 on 1 April 2013. The annual value of the house is

£1,500. Bella pays £75 a month to the employer for the use of the house. She is also provided with new furniture valued at £15,000 on 1 April 2025.

Required

(d) Complete the following sentences

(4 marks)

(i) The basic accommodation benefit for 2025/26 is:

£ ______

(ii) The cost of providing the accommodation for calculating the additional benefit is:

£ ______

(iii) The additional accommodation benefit for 2025/26 is:

£ ______

(iv) The benefit for provision of furniture for 2025/26 is:

£ ______

(e) Which TWO of the following are not a wholly exempt employment benefit?

	✓
Long service award worth £900 to employee with 30 years of service	
Workplace parking	
Workplace childcare facilities	
Moving expenses of £10,000	
Canteen available to senior management only	

(2 marks)

Task 3 (10 marks)

(a) Complete the following sentences.

(4 marks)

Sarah is a higher rate taxpayer and receives total dividends of £7,000 during 2025/26.

Required

The amount of the dividend not taxed at 0% is:

£ ______

The income tax payable on the dividend income is (to the nearest £1):

£ ______

Paul is a basic rate taxpayer and receives interest of £5,000 from an ISA and £3,500 of building society interest during 2025/26.

Required

His personal savings allowance is:

£ ______

The income tax payable on his savings income for 2025/26 is:

£ [ ]

Demi bought two properties on 1 July 2025.

Property 1 was let unfurnished from 1 September 2025 at an annual rent of £12,000 payable monthly in arrears. The rent due on 31 March 2026 was not received until 14 April 2026.

The following were expenses paid by Demi on the property:

		£
1 July 2025	Insurance for the year ended 30 June 2026	700
8 Sept 2025	Accountancy fees	100
25 January 2026	Re-painting the exterior of the property	400

Property 2 was let furnished from 1 August 2025 at an annual rent of £9,000 payable annually in advance.

The following were expenses paid by Demi on the property:

		£
1 July 2025	Insurance for the year ended 30 June 2026	800
31 March 2026	Redecoration	900
3 April 2026	Purchase of replacement carpets and curtains	600

Required

(b) Using the proforma layout provided, calculate Demi's property income for the tax year 2025/26 by filling in the unshaded boxes. Add zeros if necessary. Both brackets and minus signs can be used to show negative numbers.

	Property 1 £	Property 2 £
Rental income		
Property 1		
Property 2		
Less expenses		
Insurance		
Accountancy		
Repainting		
Redecoration		
Replacement carpets and curtains		
Net income		
Total property income 2025/26		

(4 marks)

(c) **On which expenditure could Demi claim replacement furniture relief? (Tick all that apply)**

	✓
A new fridge to replace the one that stopped working last week	
A television for the new conservatory	
New carpet for the living room after the old one was damaged in the recent floods	
New crockery for the kitchen to replace the chipped plates and bowls	

(2 marks)

Task 4 (14 marks)

Donald and Jackie received the following income in 2025/26:

	Donald £	Jackie £
Employment income (PAYE deducted £52,000)	152,395	
Property income		65,000
Building society interest	400	1,500
Interest from an ISA	500	
Dividends	1,000	2,500

Jackie has property losses brought forward of £10,000 and also made monthly payments of £200 into a private personal pension scheme.

Required

Calculate the total income tax payable for Donald and Jackie to the nearest pound for 2025/26, entering your answer and workings in the blank table given below.

(14 marks)

Task 5 (6 marks)

Sandy works for Geese Ltd. She is paid monthly and has an annual salary of £48,000. In March 2026 she received a bonus of £10,000.

Required

(a) What national insurance contributions are suffered by Sandy and her employer? Enter your answer in whole pounds only and ignore the employment allowance.

Class 1 Employee

£ [ ]

Class 1 Employer

£ [ ]

(4 marks)

(b) Identify whether the following statements are true or false

Statement	True ✓	False ✓
Duncan has two employees who earn £12,500 and £10,000. He will not have to pay employers' class 1 NIC.		
National insurance is charged on employer contributions to occupational pension schemes.		

(2 marks)

Task 6 (8 marks)

Complete the following sentences. Assume rates and allowances remain the same as 2025/26.

(8 marks)

Mr and Mrs Shah are thinking of buying a property to rent out which is expected to generate income of £10,000 per annum. Mrs Shah is a stay-at-home mum with no income and Mr Shah is a higher rate taxpayer.

Required

(i) If Mrs Shah owns the property instead of Mr Shah, the income tax saving would be:

£ [ ]

Kerry is considering getting a company car. She is looking at a car with a list price of £22,000 and a scale rate percentage of 20%. Her employer will pay for private fuel costs which are expected to total £6,000 per annum. Kerry will make a £2,000 contribution annually but can choose whether to make this towards use of the car or fuel. Kerry is a basic rate taxpayer.

Required

(ii) If Kerry makes an annual contribution towards use of the car instead of fuel, the income tax saving would be:

£ [ ]

David has employment income of £70,000. He joined his employer's occupational pension scheme on 1 April 2025. David makes annual contributions of 10% of salary and his employer contributes an additional 5%.

Required

(iii) By joining the occupational pension scheme, David has saved income tax of:

£ [ ]

Michelle's employer has loaned her £12,000 on which she pays interest of £180 annually. She wants to know how much more interest she would have to pay annually to avoid a taxable benefit.

Required

(iv) **Michelle would need to pay additional interest of:**

£ [   ]

Task 7 (10 marks)

(a) **Classify whether a disposal of each of the following assets will be chargeable to or exempt from capital gains tax:**

Asset	Chargeable ✓	Exempt ✓
Shares in XYZ plc held in an ISA		
Ruby necklace valued at £100,000		
Vintage Rolls Royce Car		
Factory used in a trade		

(4 marks)

Trevor bought a 5-acre plot of land for £50,000. He sold 3 acres of the land at auction for £105,000 in August 2025. He had spent £2,500 installing drainage on the 3 acres which he sold. His disposal costs were £1,500. The market value of the remaining 2 acres at the date of sale was £45,000.

Required

(b) **Complete the following sentences**

(4 marks)

(i) **The allowable cost of the land is:**

	✓
£52,500	
£37,500	
£32,500	
£36,750	

(ii) **The gain on sale of the land is:**

	✓
£66,000	
£66,750	
£67,500	
£70,000	

(c) **Complete the following sentences**

(2 marks)

Matt bought a picture for £7,000 and had costs of acquisition of £300. He sold it in August 2025 for £4,500 and had costs of disposal of £200.

Required

(i) The allowable loss on sale is: (either show the loss by using brackets or a minus sign)

£ [ ]

Keith bought a greyhound for £5,000. It won a number of races and he sold it for £7,000 in December 2025, incurring costs of disposal of £250.

Required

(ii) The chargeable gain on sale is:

	✓
Nil	
£1,667	
£1,250	
£1,750	

Task 8 (8 marks)

Lee had the following transactions in shares in Snowy Ltd:

Acquisitions	No of shares	Cost £
December 2008	10,000	10,800
August 2009	Bonus, 1 for 1	Nil
June 2013	10,000	8,700
December 2013	Rights Issue, 1 for 10	40p each

Disposal		Proceeds £
September 2025	15,000	18,650

Required

Calculate the chargeable gain made on the disposal of the shares in Snowy Ltd, and show the balance of shares to be carried forward for future disposal. Fill in all unshaded boxes, enter 0 if appropriate. Both brackets and minus signs can be used to show negative numbers.

Gain

	£

Share pool

	No of shares	Cost £

(8 marks)

Task 9 (10 marks)

(a) For each of the following statements, tick if they are True or False.

	True ✓	False ✓
Brought forward losses are deducted after the annual exempt amount.		
A taxpayer can leave their main residence before it is sold and still claim full private residence relief.		
Spouses and civil partners share one annual exempt amount between them.		
A basic rate taxpayer pays capital gains tax at 24%.		

(4 marks)

On 1 March 2004, Craig bought a house for £36,000. He lived in it until 1 September 2007, when he went to Australia to take up employment. He returned from there on 1 September 2013 and moved back into the house until 1 March 2019 when he purchased a small flat. He has lived in the flat since then. Craig finally sold the house for £178,000 on 31 August 2025.

Required

(b) Complete the following sentences

(4 marks)

(i) The number of exempt months are:

[ ] months

(ii) The chargeable gain on the sale is:

£ [ ]

Irma had the following chargeable gains in 2025/26:

Gain on sale of shares August 2025	£9,341
Gain on sale of furniture February 2026	£4,167
She had allowable losses brought forward of	£1,000

Irma has £170,000 of employment income.

Required

(c) Complete the following sentences

(2 marks)

(i) Irma's taxable gains for 2025/26 are:

£ [ ]

(ii) Irma's CGT payable for 2025/26 is:

£ [ ]

Task 10 (10 marks)

(a) Identify whether the following statements are true or false.

	True ✓	False ✓
IHT on the death estate is payable by the recipients.		
The residence nil rate band is available for a gift to children or grandchildren.		
Ugo makes a gift to his daughter of £4,000 on occasion of her marriage. This is exempt from IHT.		
When considering the death tax on a lifetime gift you need to look at transfers in the seven years before the date of death in order to calculate the nil rate band available.		
A gift of cash to a sibling may only become taxable on death of the donor.		

(5 marks)

Gillian owned a 70% shareholding in R Ltd, an unquoted investment company. On 23 July 2025, she gave a 20% shareholding in R Ltd to her son. The values of shareholdings in R Ltd on 23 July 2025 were as follows:

	£
100% shareholding	600,000
70% shareholding	350,000
50% shareholding	200,000
20% shareholding	80,000

Required

(b) What is the diminution in value of Gillian's estate as a result of her gift on 23 July 2025?

	✓
£150,000	
£270,000	
£80,000	
£120,000	

(1 mark)

Mary made the following gifts in the tax year 2025/26:

(1) £1,000 to her local Green political party.

(2) £200 to her grandson on his birthday and a further £250 to the same grandson as a Christmas gift.

Required

(c) Ignoring the annual exemption, what is the total value of potentially exempt transfers made by Mary as a result of these gifts?

	✓
£1,450	
£250	
£1,000	
£450	

(1 mark)

Duncan makes only the following gifts in 2025/26.

Required

(d) Are these PETs or exempt transfers?

Date/Gift	PET ✓	Exempt ✓
01.06.25 Gift of shares worth £3,000 to his cousin		
08.08.25 Gift of investment property to charity		
23.02.26 Gift of car worth £50,000 to his daughter		

(3 marks)

BPP Practice Assessment 2

Personal Tax FA 2025

Answers

Task 1

(a) Firstly, it needs to be established whether this information is correct. Then, if this information is correct, the client needs to be approached.

If the client confirms this information to be correct and agrees to disclose this income to HMRC then the client needs to be advised of any penalties, interest, and other consequences.

If the client refuses to disclose this income to HMRC then you must cease to act for the client and inform HMRC that you no longer act for the client. However, because of the fundamental principle of confidentiality you would not need to disclose the reason for ceasing to act to HMRC.

This may be a money laundering issue and so this should be reported to your Money Laundering Officer

(b) To maintain professional knowledge and skill at the level required to ensure that a client or employer receives competent professional service based on current developments in practice, legislation and techniques and acts diligently and in accordance with applicable technical and professional standards.

Professional competence and due care

(c) Confidentiality

Task 2

(a) **(i)** 24 %

17% + (90 – 55)/5%

(ii) £ 1,932

£13,800 × 24% × 7/12

(iii) £ 1,232

(£13,800 - £5,000) × 24% × 7/12

£5,000 is the maximum capital contribution.

(iv) £ 3,948

£28,200 × 24% × 7/12

(b) Matthew is provided with a company van for the whole of 2025/26. The only private use of the van is the commute from home to work.

The taxable benefit for use of the van is:

£ Nil

Luke is provided with a company van on 6 April 2025 which he uses for both personal and business purposes. The company pays for all of the fuel. He was made redundant on 6 October 2025, and he returned the van to the company on that date.

The taxable benefit for use of the van and private fuel is:

£ 2,395

(£4,020 + £769) × 6/12

ANSWERS

(c) (i) £ 0

No taxable benefit arises if the combined outstanding balance on all loans to the employee did not exceed £10,000 at any time in the tax year.

(ii) £ 0

Exempt

(d) (i) £ 600

	£
Annual value	1,500
Less payment by employee £75 × 12 =	(900)
Basic accommodation benefit	600

(ii) £ 125,000

Market value at provision (acquired more than 6 years before provision)

(iii) £ 1,875

Excess of £125,000 over £75,000 = £50,000 × 3.75%

(iv) £ 3,000

£15,000 × 20%

(e) The correct answers are:

	✓
Long service award worth £900 to employee with 30 years of service	
Workplace parking	
Workplace childcare facilities	
Moving expenses of £10,000	✓
Canteen available to senior management only	✓

Moving expenses of £10,000 are only exempt up to £8,000, the excess is taxable.

The long service award is wholly exempt as it is within the limit of £50 for each year of service and the period of service is in excess of 20 years.

Provision of a canteen is only exempt if it is available to all staff.

Task 3

(a) (i) The amount of the dividend not taxed at 0% is:

£ 6,500

The income tax payable on the dividend income is (to the nearest £1):

£ 2,194

£7,000 – £500

£6,500 × 33.75% (higher rate taxpayer)

(ii) His personal savings allowance is:

£ 1,000

The income tax payable on his savings income for 2025/26 is:

£ 500

Paul is a basic rate taxpayer.

£2,500 × 20% = £500

The ISA income is exempt.

(b)

	Property 1 £	Property 2 £
Rental income		
Property 1 £12,000/12 × 6	6,000	
Property 2		9,000
Less expenses		
Insurance	(700)	(800)
Accountancy	(100)	0
Repainting	(400)	0
Redecoration	0	(900)
Replacement carpets and curtains	0	(600)
Net income	4,800	6,700
Total property income 2025/26	11,500	

(c) The correct answers are:

	✓
A new fridge to replace the one that stopped working last week	✓
A television for the new conservatory	
New carpet for the living room after the old one was damaged in the recent floods	✓
New crockery for the kitchen to replace the chipped plates and bowls	✓

The television is not a replacement as the conservatory is new and therefore, there would not have been one there before.

Task 4

	Non-savings £	Interest £	Dividends £
Donald			
Employment Income	152,395		
Building society interest		400	
ISA interest (exempt)		0	
Dividends			1,000
Net income	152,395	400	1,000
Personal allowance (fully abated as net income >£125,140)	0		
Taxable income	152,395	400	1,000
£37,700 × 20%	7,540		
£87,440 (£125,140 – £37,700) × 40%	34,976		
£27,255 (£152,395 – £125,140) × 45%	12,265		
£Nil × 0% (additional rate taxpayer)	0		
£400 × 45%	180		
£500 × 0%	0		
£500 × 39.35%	197		
Income tax liability	55,158		
PAYE	(52,000)		
Income tax payable	3,158		
Jackie			
Property income	65,000		
Property loss	(10,000)		
Building society interest		1,500	
Dividends			2,500
Net income	55,000	1,500	2,500
Personal allowance	(12,570)		
Taxable income	42,430	1,500	2,500
£37,700 × 20%	7,540		

	Non-savings £	Interest £	Dividends £
£3,000 × 20% (100/80 × £200 × 12)	600		
£1,730 (£42,430 – £37,700 – £3,000) × 40%	692		
£500 × 0%	0		
£1,000 × 40%	400		
£500 × 0%	0		
£2,000 × 33.75%	675		
Income tax liability/payable	9,907		

Task 5

(a) Class 1 Employee

£ 3,045

Class 1 Employer

£ 7,950

Working

£(48,000/12) = £4,000 per month	
£(4,000 – 1,048) = 2,952 × 8% × 11 months =	2,598
£(4,189 – 1,048) = 3,141 × 8% × 1 month =	251
£(14,000 – 4,189) = 9,811 × 2% × 1 month =	196
	3,045

£58,000 – £5,000 = £53,000 × 15% = £7,950

(b) The correct answers are:

Statement	True ✓	False ✓
Duncan has two employees who earn £12,500 and £10,000. He will not have to pay employers' class 1 NIC. **Explanation:** Employment allowance reduces employer's class 1 to nil.	✓	
National insurance is charged on employer contributions to occupational pension schemes.		✓

Task 6

(i) £ 400

£10,000 × 40%. The rental income would be fully covered by Mrs Shah's personal allowance.

(ii) £ 400

£2,000 × 20%. The fuel benefit is not reduced by a partial contribution.

(iii) £ 2,800

£7,000 × 40%

(iv) £ 270

(3.75% × £12,000) – £180

Task 7

(a) The correct answers are:

Asset	Chargeable ✓	Exempt ✓
Shares in XYZ plc held in an ISA		✓
Ruby necklace valued at £100,000	✓	
Vintage Rolls Royce Car		✓
Factory used in a trade	✓	

(b) **(i)** The correct answer is:

	✓
£52,500	
£37,500	✓
£32,500	
£36,750	

(ii) The correct answer is:

	✓
£66,000	✓
£66,750	
£67,500	
£70,000	

	£
Proceeds of sale	105,000
Less costs of disposal	(1,500)
Net proceeds	103,500
Less cost	
(105,000/105,000 + 45,000) × £50,000	(35,000)
enhancement expenditure	(2,500)
Chargeable gain	66,000

The answer £52,500 is the cost without adjustment for part disposal. The answer £32,500 uses 3/5 acres as the fraction in the part disposal calculation. The answer £36,750 applies the part disposal calculation to both the original cost and enhancement expenditure.

The answer £66,750 calculates the part disposal on cost plus enhancement expenditure. The answer £67,500 ignores costs of disposal. The answer £70,000 ignores costs and enhancement expenditure.

(c) (i) £ (1,500)

	£
Deemed disposal proceeds	6,000
Less costs of disposal	(200)
Net deemed disposal proceeds	5,800
Less cost £(7,000 + 300)	(7,300)
Allowable loss	(1,500)

(ii) The correct answer is:

	✓
Nil	✓
£1,667	
£1,250	
£1,750	

The greyhound is a wasting chattel and so is an exempt asset. Therefore, there is no chargeable gain on the disposal.

Task 8

Gain

	£
Proceeds of sale	18,650
Less cost	(9,409)
Chargeable gain	9,241

Share pool

	No of shares	Cost £
December 2008 Acquisition	10,000	10,800
August 2009 Bonus 1 for 1	10,000	0
	20,000	10,800
June 2013 Acquisition	10,000	8,700

	No of shares	Cost £
	30,000	19,500
December 2013 Rights 1 for 10 × £0.40	3,000	1,200
	33,000	20,700
September 2025 Disposal (15,000/33,000 × £20,700)	(15,000)	(9,409)
c/f	18,000	11,291

Task 9

(a) The correct answers are:

	True ✓	False ✓
Brought forward losses are deducted after the annual exempt amount. **Explanation:** (current year losses are deducted before)	✓	
A taxpayer can leave their main residence before it is sold and still claim full private residence relief. **Explanation:** (last nine months always exempt)	✓	
Spouses and civil partners share one annual exempt amount between them. **Explanation:** (each individual has their own AEA)		✓
A basic rate taxpayer pays capital gains tax at 24%. **Explanation:** CGT is 18% in the basic rate band.		✓

(b) **(i)** 189 months

Working

Time period	Chargeable months	Exempt months	Total months
1.3.04 to 31.8.07		42	42
1.9.07 to 31.8.13 (Note. 1)		72	72
1.9.13 to 28.02.19		66	66
1.03.19 to 31.08.25 (Note. 2)	69	9	78
	69	189	258

Notes.

1 Any period of employment abroad is treated as deemed occupation if it is preceded and followed by actual occupation.

2 Last nine months of ownership is always exempt if the property has been the taxpayer's only or main residence at some time during the ownership period.

(ii) £ 37,977

Chargeable gain on sale of property	£
Proceeds of sale	178,000
Less allowable cost	(36,000)
Gain before PRR	142,000
Less PRR exempt amount ((189/258) × 142,000)	(104,023)
Chargeable gain	37,977

(c) (i) £ 9,508

	£
Gain on shares	9,341
Gain on furniture	4,167
Net chargeable gains	13,508
Less annual exempt amount	(3,000)
Less loss brought forward	(1,000)
Taxable gains	9,508

(ii) £ 2,282

£9,508 × 24%

Task 10

(a) The correct answers are:

	True ✓	False ✓
IHT on the death estate is payable by the recipients. **Explanation:** (paid by executors)		✓
The residence nil rate band is available for a gift to children or grandchildren. **Explanation:** (direct descendants)	✓	
Ugo makes a gift to his daughter of £4,000 on occasion of her marriage. This is exempt from IHT. **Explanation:** (up to £5,000 where a parent)	✓	
When considering the death tax on a lifetime gift you need to look at transfers in the seven years before the date of death in order to calculate the nil rate band available. **Explanation:** (seven years prior to gift)		✓

ANSWERS

	True ✓	False ✓
A gift of cash to a sibling may only become taxable on death of the donor. **Explanation:** (PET)	✓	

(b) The correct answer is:

	✓
£150,000	✓
£270,000	
£80,000	
£120,000	

Working

	£
Before the gift: 70% shareholding	350,000
After the gift: 50% shareholding	(200,000)
Transfer of value	150,000

The answer £270,000 is the value of a 70% shareholding less the value of a 20% shareholding. The answer £80,000 is the value of a 20% shareholding. The answer £120,000 is 20% of the value of a 100% holding.

(c) The correct answer is:

	✓
£1,450	
£250	
£1,000	
£450	✓

Working

Gifts to political parties are exempt.

The small gifts exemption only applies to gifts up to £250 per donee, per tax year. If gifts total more than £250 the whole amount is chargeable. Since the gifts to the grandson totalled £(200 + 250) = £450 in 2025/26, this exemption does not apply.

(d) The correct answers are:

Date/Gift	PET ✓	Exempt ✓
01.06.25 Gift of shares worth £3,000 to his cousin **Explanation:** (covered by annual exemption)		✓
08.08.25 Gift of investment property to charity		✓

Date/Gift	PET ✓	Exempt ✓
23.02.26 Gift of car worth £50,000 to his daughter **Explanation:** (cars only exempt from CGT)	✓	

BPP Practice Assessment 3

Personal Tax FA 2025

Time allowed: 2 hours 30 minutes

Personal Tax FA 2025

BPP Practice Assessment 3

Assessment information

You have **2 1/2 hours** to complete this sample assessment.

- This assessment contains **10 tasks** and you should attempt to complete every task.
- Each task is independent. You will not need to refer to your answers in previous tasks.
- The total number of marks for this assessment is 100.
- Read every task carefully to make sure you understand what is required.
- Where the date is relevant, it is given in the task data.
- Both minus signs or brackets can be used to indicate negative numbers **unless** task instructions say otherwise.
- You must use a full stop to indicate a decimal point. For example, write 100.57 NOT 100,57 or 100 57.
- You may use a comma to indicate a number in the thousands, but you don't have to. For example, 10000 and 10,000 are both acceptable.
- If your answer requires rounding, apply normal mathematical rules **unless** the task instructions say otherwise

In the live assessment you will have access to the tax tables and reference material which have been reproduced at the back of this Question Bank. Please use them while completing this practice assessment so that you are familiar with their content.

Task 1 (10 marks)

You receive the following email from a client, who is a higher rate taxpayer.

To:	AATStudent@boxmail.net
From:	Raman99@sherbet.net
Date:	20 June 2026
Subject:	More information

Hello, I am so sorry, I know that you have already sent in my tax form for 2025/26. Unfortunately, I forgot to tell you that I started letting out a property on 1 January 2026 and received £3,000 of rental income for the first three months.

I suggest we leave the 2025/26 return as it is, and I will just account for the income as if I started renting the property in April 2026.

Thanks.

Raman

Required

(a) Reply to Raman's email.

To: Raman99@sherbet.net

From: AATStudent@boxmail.net

Date: 22 June 2026

Subject: More information

(6 marks)

One of your clients, Flavia, is considering moving to the UK with their spouse. Flavia was born in Italy and has lived there all her life however, following her retirement, she would like to live in the UK for a couple of years, after which she will return to Italy. Flavia intends to buy a house to live in the UK. She will not work whilst in the UK but will receive property income from her global portfolio. Flavia has not previously visited the UK.

Required

(b) Explain:

(4 marks)

(i) How many days Flavia would need to spend in the UK in 2025/26 to be considered UK tax resident.

(ii) **Explain how Flavia will be taxed if she becomes UK resident, and how that will differ once she becomes non-UK resident again.**

Task 2 (14 marks)

Khalid works for KML plc and is provided with a company car for business and private use from 6 June 2025.

The car has CO_2 emissions of 112 g/km and has a list price of £27,000, although the company actually paid £23,500 for the car. Khalid agreed to make a capital contribution of £6,000 towards the cost of the car. The company pays for all running costs, including all fuel. Khalid pays £50 a month towards the cost of private fuel – the actual cost of private fuel is about £90 a month.

Required

(a) Complete the following sentences

(6 marks)

(i) **The cost of the car in the taxable benefit computation is:**

	✓
£21,000	
£22,000	
£17,500	
£18,500	

(ii) **The percentage used in the taxable benefit computation is:**

[ ] %

(iii) **The taxable benefit in respect of the provision of fuel for private use is:**

£ [ ]

(iv) **If an electric car costing £24,000 (same as the list price) with CO2 emissions of 45g/km and an electric mileage range of 55 miles, was provided to an employee on the 6 April 2025, the company car benefit for 2025/26 would be:**

£ [ ]

Lou is employed by Jane Quentin and receives the following benefits as a result of her employment.

Required

(b) In each case enter the taxable benefit arising. Enter 0 if the benefit is not taxable.

(4 marks)

(i) **An interest free loan of £10,500 made on 1 July 2025, no repayments made during 2025/26.**

£ [ ]

(ii) **Cash voucher for £100 provided in December 2025. Jane acquired the voucher for £90.**

£ [ ]

(iii) **Van for business and private use from 1 October 2025 onwards.**

£ [ ]

(iv) **Fuel for van for private use from 1 January 2026 onwards.**

£ [ ]

(c) **For each of the following benefits, tick whether they would be partly exempt or wholly exempt if received by an employee who is a basic rate taxpayer in 2025/26:**

Benefit	Partly exempt ✓	Wholly exempt ✓
Staff party costing £125 per head		
Mobile phone		
Removal expenses of £10,000		

(3 marks)

Madge is employed by V plc. She uses her own car for business purposes and is reimbursed 45p per mile by her employer. Madge travelled 15,000 miles on business in 2025/26.

Required

(d) **What are the employment income consequences of the reimbursement for business mileage?**

	✓
£6,750 taxable benefit	
£1,000 taxable benefit	
No taxable benefit or allowable deduction	
£1,000 allowable deduction	

(1 mark)

Task 3 (10 marks)

A higher rate taxpayer receives £3,250 of bank interest, £250 of which was from their cash ISA, and £9,500 of dividends during 2025/26.

Required

(a) What amounts will be liable to income tax at a rate of above 0% in 2025/26?

	✓
£3,000 of interest and £9,000 of dividends	
£2,500 of interest and £10,000 of dividends	
£2,250 of interest and £9,000 of dividends	
£2,500 of interest and £9,000 of dividends	

(2 marks)

Marcello receives a dividend of £4,900 in March 2026. He is an additional rate taxpayer.

Required

(b) Complete the following sentences

(2 marks)

(i) The amount of the dividend that Marcello will pay income tax on at a rate greater than 0% is:

£ ______

(ii) The tax payable on the dividend is:

£ ______

Wilma owns two flats that she rents out. Flat A is unfurnished. Flat B is furnished. She has chosen to use the accruals basis to calculate her property profits.

The income and expenses for these properties are

	Flat A £	Flat B £
Monthly income:		
Rent	500	650
Annual expenses:		
Council tax	1,000	800
Water rates	300	300
Insurance	350	250

Flat A was fully occupied during 2025/26. However, the tenants in Flat B moved out in November 2025 having paid the rent to the end of that month. Wilma was unable to re-let the flat until June 2026.

Wilma spent £410 replacing various items of furniture for Flat B that had been damaged by the outgoing tenants.

Wilma had a loss of £1,200 on her income from property in 2024/25.

Required

(c) Calculate Wilma's property income for 2025/26. Enter 0 if appropriate. Both brackets and minus signs can be used to show negative numbers.

	Flat A £	Flat B £

(4 marks)

(d) **Tick the relevant box to show which of the following types of income are chargeable to income tax and which are exempt from income tax:**

Source of income	Chargeable ✓	Exempt ✓
Property income of £850		
Government stock interest		
Dividends received from an Individual Savings Account		
Bank deposit account interest		

(2 marks)

Task 4 (14 marks)

Guy has the following income for 2025/26:

	£
Employment income (PAYE £14,108)	72,000
Interest received from building societies	30,000
Dividends received	14,000

Guy pays 8% of his salary into an occupational pension scheme and his employer pays an additional 3%. Guy's employer also pays for his private gym membership which is worth £600 annually but cost his employer £450 due to a bulk discount.

Required

(a) **Calculate Guy's income tax payable for 2025/26 entering your answer and workings into the blank table below. Brackets or a minus sign are both acceptable when entering negative numbers.**

(11 marks)

Guy is considering making a small charitable donation of about £600 a year either personally or through his workplace giving scheme but is unsure if he will get any tax relief for this.

Required

(b) Explain to Guy how he will get tax relief on such donations.

(3 marks)

Task 5 (6 marks)

Sarah has a salary of £56,000. She also has the use of a company car with a taxable benefit of £3,850.

Required

(a) What national insurance contributions are suffered by Sarah and her employer?

(4 marks)

(i) Class 1 Employee

£ ____

(ii) Class 1 Employer

£ ____

(iii) Class 1A

£ ____

(b) Identify whether the following statements are true or false

	True ✓	False ✓
Employer pension contributions to occupational pension schemes are subject to national insurance contributions.		
The employment allowance is available to employers who carry out functions of a public nature, for example the provision of services in the National Health Service.		

(2 marks)

Task 6 (8 marks)

Owen is employed by X Ltd throughout 2025/26. He earns £55,000 a year. He also receives interest income from a Santander Bank current account.

Required

(a) Owen could do the following to save tax:

	True ✓	False ✓
Invest his savings in an ISA		

	True ✓	False ✓
Donate to charity under the Gift Aid scheme		
Invest in a property		
Contribute to a pension		

(4 marks)

(b) **Complete the following sentences.**

(4 marks)

In 2025/26 Mustafah received property income of £3,000 and incurred allowable property expenses of £400. He also received income from his employment of £60,000.

Required

(i) **If Mustafah elects to use the property allowance, he will save income tax of:**

£ [ ]

In 2025/26 Ginny was employed with a salary of £170,000. She also has use of a car from her employer with a list price of £35,000 and a taxable benefit of £7,700.

Required

(ii) **If the car had been an electric car with CO_2 emissions of 40g/km and an electric mileage range of 36 miles, this would have saved Ginny income tax of:**

£ [ ]

Task 7 (10 marks)

(a) **For each statement, tick the appropriate box in respect of the capital gains calculation.**

Disposal	Market value used ✓	Actual proceeds used ✓	No gain/no loss disposal ✓
Olivia sells shares for £5,000 to her wife Lucy when they are worth £4,000			
William sells land to his brother for £10,000 when it is worth £50,000			
Zeta gives an asset worth £4,000 to her friend Tanya			
Olwyn sells listed shares for proceeds of £12,000			

(4 marks)

(b) **Complete the following sentences**

(6 marks)

Ulma bought a holiday cottage for £65,000 and spent £15,000 on an extension and £10,000 on redecoration. She sold the cottage for £125,000 on 10 August 2025.

Required

(i) **The chargeable gain on sale is:**

£ [ ]

Jade purchased an emerald bracelet for £8,000. She sold the bracelet in August 2025 at auction for £2,700 (which was net of 10% commission).

Required

(ii) The allowable loss on sale is:

£ [ ]

James sold a table in February 2026 for £5,900 which he had purchased 4 years before for £4,500.

Required

(iii) The chargeable gain on sale is:

£ [ ]

Sinead sold a classic car for £350,000 which she had bought for £100,000 incurring legal fees of £8,500.

Required

(iv) The chargeable gain on sale is:

£ [ ]

Lionel sold 2 acres of land in September 2025 for £125,000. Auctioneers' commission was 1%. The original 10 acres had cost him £70,000 in June 2003. The remaining 8 acres had a market value of £375,000 at the date of sale.

Required

(v) The allowable cost is:

£ [ ]

The chargeable gain on sale is:

£ [ ]

Task 8 (8 marks)

Vernon sold 4,000 shares in R Ltd for £36,200 on 23 February 2026. He had acquired his holdings in R Ltd as follows:

Date	Transaction	No of shares	£
14 April 2003	Purchase	6,000	18,400
29 May 2008	Rights issue	1 for 20	£4 each
10 March 2026	Purchase	500	3,400

Required

Using the proforma layout provided, compute the total gain on sale. Both brackets and minus signs can be used to show negative numbers.

Share pool

	No of shares	Cost £

	No of shares	Cost £

Total gain on sale

	£

(8 marks)

Task 9 (10 marks)

Desmond bought a house in Glasgow on 1 April 2009. He lived in the house until 30 September 2012. He was then sent to work in Bristol by his employer, before returning to live in the house again on 1 October 2017. He lived in the house before moving out on 30 April 2018 to live with friends until the house was sold on 30 September 2025.

Required

(a) Using the proforma layout provided, show which periods of ownership are exempt and which are chargeable matching the correct explanation for each period.

Explanation	Exempt (dates)	Chargeable (dates)
(1) ▼	(2) ▼	▼
(1) ▼	(2) ▼	▼
(1) ▼	(2) ▼	▼
(1) ▼	(2) ▼	▼
(1) ▼	▼	(2) ▼
(1) ▼	(2) ▼	▼

Picklist 1

- Actual occupation
- Four years employed elsewhere in UK
- Last nine months ownership
- Not occupied and not followed by actual occupation
- Up to three years any reason

Picklist 2

- 1 April 2009 to 30 September 2012
- 1 January 2025 to 30 September 2025
- 1 May 2018 to 31 December 2024
- 1 October 2012 to 30 September 2016
- 1 October 2016 to 30 September 2017
- 1 October 2017 to 30 April 2018

(5 marks)

(b) Complete the following sentences

(5 marks)

During 2025/26 Nina sold an asset giving rise to a chargeable gain of £18,000. She has capital losses brought forward at 6 April 2025 of £19,000.

Required

(i) The amount of capital losses Nina will have to carry forward at 5 April 2026 is:

£ [ ]

Jai makes chargeable gains (on antiques) of £14,000 in November 2025. Jai's taxable income for 2025/26 is £37,090 and he made a Gift Aid payment of £400 to Oxfam in May 2025. Jai has a loss brought forward from 2024/25 of £1,000.

Required

(ii) Calculate the following:

Jai's taxable gain for 2025/26 is:

£ [ ]

The CGT payable for 2025/26 is:

£ [ ]

Task 10 (10 marks)

(a) Identify whether the following statements are true or false

	True ✓	False ✓
The taper relief for an individual who survives four but not five years from the date of the gift is 40%.		
Where lifetime tax is paid on CLTs by the donor it is calculated at 20%.		
Marriage exemptions are only available where the gift is made to relatives.		

	True ✓	False ✓
The annual exemption for the year of the death may be deducted from the death estate.		
The residence nil rate band is not available on lifetime transfers.		

(5 marks)

(b) Complete the following sentences

(3 marks)

On 9 September 2025 Jimmy gave 200 shares valued at £5 each in J Ltd, an unquoted investment company, to his daughter. Before the gift, Jimmy owned 5,100 shares valued at £30 each in J Ltd. After the gift Jimmy owned 4,900 shares valued at £20 each in J Ltd.

Required

(i) The diminution in value in Jimmy's estate as a result of his gift is:

	✓
£55,000	
£4,000	
£6,000	
£1,000	

On 2 August 2025 Jacinta made a cash gift to her grandson of £10,000 as a wedding gift when he got married. Jacinta has not previously made any other gifts.

Required

(ii) The total amount of the exemptions that may be deducted in computing the PET are:

	✓
£3,000	
£8,500	
£6,000	
£11,000	

Rodney died on 13 August 2025 leaving an estate worth £520,000. In his will he left £200 in cash to each of his five nephews, investments held in ISAs valued at £350,000 to his daughter, and the residue of his estate to his wife.

Required

(iii) The chargeable estate is:

	✓
£520,000	
£351,000	
£350,000	
£1,000	

Devika makes the following gifts in 2025/26.

Required

(c) Complete the table below to show whether these gifts would be an exempt transfer or a potentially exempt transfer.

Gift	Date	Status
Cash to the Conservative political party of £3,000	1 October 2025	▼
Shares to her daughter worth £2,700	26 February 2026	▼

Picklist

- Exempt
- Potentially exempt

(2 marks)

BPP Practice Assessment 3

Personal Tax FA 2025

Answers

Task 1

(a)

> To: Raman99@sherbet.net
>
> From: AATStudent@boxmail.net
>
> Date: 22 June 2026
>
> Subject: More information
>
> Thank you for your email. Unfortunately, I cannot condone the action you have suggested as it amounts to tax evasion. By not declaring the income you are deliberately misleading HMRC resulting in an underpayment of your tax in 2025/26. Should they choose to look into your tax return and discover this omission you would be liable to interest and penalties.
>
> Ultimately it is your choice and I can only advise you as to the correct course of action. However, if you choose not to take my advice then I would have to cease acting for you with regard to your tax affairs and inform HMRC that I have done so. I will not tell them why as this would be a breach of client confidentiality.
>
> I hope it doesn't come to this. Please feel free to contact me to discuss this matter.

(b) **(i)** Flavia has not previously been UK tax resident. Therefore, she will only be considered UK tax resident if she spends over 120 days in the UK. This is because she will have two ties to the UK (close family and accommodation).

(ii) In the tax years that Flavia is UK resident, she will be taxed in the UK on her worldwide income and gains on an arising basis, regardless of where the income/assets is/are located.

Once Flavia becomes non-UK resident again, she will only pay tax in the UK on her UK income and UK gains. Any overseas income and gains will be exempt from income tax and capital gains tax.

Task 2

(a) **(i)** The correct answer is:

	✓
£21,000	
£22,000	✓
£17,500	
£18,500	

List price £27,000 less capital contribution paid by employee (max) £5,000

The answer £21,000 deducts the total capital contribution paid. The answer £17,500 uses the amount actually paid less the total contribution. The answer £18,500 uses the amount actually paid less the restricted contribution.

(ii) 28 %

17% + (110 – 55)/5% = 28%

(iii) £ 6,580

£28,200 × 28% × 10/12 (There is no reduction for part reimbursement of private fuel).

(iv) £ 2,160

CO_2 emissions less than 50g/km and mileage range 40 to 69 is 9%

ANSWERS

9% × £24,000

(b) **(i)** £ 295

£10,500 × 3.75% × 9/12

(ii) £ 100

(iii) £ 2,010

£4,020 × 6/12

(iv) £ 192

£769 × 3/12

(c) The correct answers are:

Benefit	Partly exempt ✓	Wholly exempt ✓
Staff party costing £125 per head		✓
Mobile phone		✓
Removal expenses of £10,000 **Explanation:** (up to £8,000)	✓	

(d) The correct answer is:

	✓
£6,750 taxable benefit	
£1,000 taxable benefit	✓
No taxable benefit or allowable deduction	
£1,000 allowable deduction	

Working

	£
Amount reimbursed 15,000 × 45p	6,750
Less statutory allowance	
10,000 miles × 45p	(4,500)
5,000 miles × 25p	(1,250)
Taxable benefit	1,000

Task 3

(a) The correct answer is:

	✓
£3,000 of interest and £9,000 of dividends	
£2,500 of interest and £10,000 of dividends	
£2,250 of interest and £9,000 of dividends	
£2,500 of interest and £9,000 of dividends	✓

The taxable interest is after deduction of the savings allowance (£500 for higher rate taxpayers) and excludes the ISA interest. £3,250 – £250 – £500 = £2,500. The first £500 of dividends are taxable at 0% for all taxpayers.

(b) **(i)** £ 4,400

£4,900 – £500 dividend allowance

(ii) £ 1,731

£4,400 × 39.35%

(c)

	Flat A £	Flat B £
Income: £500 × 12/ £650 × 8	6,000	5,200
Expenses:		
Council tax	(1,000)	(800)
Water rates	(300)	(300)
Insurance	(350)	(250)
Replacement furniture relief	(0)	(410)
Net income from property	4,350	3,440
Total property income £(4,350 + 3,440)	7,790	
Less loss b/f	(1,200)	
Taxable property income	6,590	

(d) The correct answers are:

Source of income	Chargeable ✓	Exempt ✓
Property income of £850 **Explanation:** (property allowance)		✓
Government stock interest	✓	
Dividends received from an Individual Savings Account		✓
Bank deposit account interest	✓	

ANSWERS

Task 4

(a)

	Non savings income £	Savings income £	Dividend income £
Employment income	72,000		
Employee pension contribution	(5,760)		
Employer pension contribution (exempt)	0		
Gym benefit	450		
Building society interest		30,000	
Dividends			14,000
Net income	66,690	30,000	14,000
Personal allowance (Working)	(7,225)		
Taxable income	59,465	30,000	14,000
Income tax			
£37,700 × 20%			7,540
£21,765 (£59,465 – £37,700) × 40%			8,706
£500 × 0% (savings allowance)			0
£29,500 (£30,000 – £500) × 40%			11,800
£500 × 0%			0
£13,500 × 33.75%			4,556
Income tax liability			32,602
Less tax deducted at source:			
PAYE			(14,108)
Income tax payable			18,494
Working - PA abatement			
Personal allowance	12,570		
Abatement (1/2 × (110,690 – 100,000)	(5,345)		
	7,225		

(b) Personal gift aid payments are deemed to be made net of 20%. Therefore, Guy would only need to make a payment of £480 for the charity to receive £600 (the £480 is grossed up by 100/80 and the charity is able to claim the additional £120).

In addition, as Guy is a higher rate taxpayer his basic rate band would be extended by the gross amount ie £600 which would save him tax of £120 (as £600 of his non-savings income would be taxable at 20% instead of 40%).

If Guy made the donation through a workplace giving scheme, his employer would deduct the donation from his salary before it is taxed. This would reduce his taxable employment income by £600, saving tax at 40% given he is a higher rate taxpayer ie a tax saving of £240.

Task 5

(a) **(i)** £ 3,131

Workings £(50,270 – 12,570) × 8% + £(56,000 – 50,270) × 2%

(ii) £ 7,650

Workings £(56,000 – 5,000) × 15%

(iii) £ 578

Workings £3,850 × 15%

(b) The correct answers are:

	True ✓	False ✓
Employer pension contributions to occupational pension schemes are subject to national insurance contributions.		✓
The employment allowance is available to employers who carry out functions of a public nature, for example the provision of services in the National Health Service. **Explanation:** (employers who carry out such functions are excluded employers)		✓

Task 6

(a) The correct answers are:

	True ✓	False ✓
Invest his savings in an ISA	✓	
Donate to charity under the Gift Aid scheme	✓	
Invest in a property		✓
Contribute to a pension	✓	

*Investing in a property would not save tax as the rental income would be taxable as non-savings income.

(b) **(i)** £ 240

(£1,000 – £400) × 40%

(ii) £ 1,418

Scale charge percentage of current car is 22% (£7,700/£35,000)

The electric car would have a scale charge percentage of 13% and therefore the taxable benefit percentage would be reduced by 9% (22% - 13%) if an electric car.

9% × £35,000 × 45% = £1,418

Task 7

(a) The correct answers are:

Disposal	Market value used ✓	Actual proceeds used ✓	No gain/no loss disposal ✓
Olivia sells shares for £5,000 to her wife Lucy when they are worth £4,000			✓
William sells land to his brother for £10,000 when it is worth £50,000	✓		
Zeta gives an asset worth £4,000 to her friend Tanya	✓		
Olwyn sells listed shares for proceeds of £12,000		✓	

(b) **(i)** £ 45,000

Proceeds of sale	125,000
Less cost	(65,000)
enhancement expenditure	(15,000)
Chargeable gain	45,000

Redecoration is a revenue expense, not capital, and therefore not allowable.

(ii) £ 2,300

Deemed disposal proceeds	6,000
Less disposal costs £2,700 × 10/90	(300)
Net proceeds	5,700
Less cost	(8,000)
Allowable loss	(2,300)

(iii) £ 0

Chattels which are bought and sold for less than £6,000 are exempt from capital gains tax.

(iv) £ 0

Cars are exempt from capital gains tax

(v) £ 17,500

The chargeable gain on sale is:

£ 106,250

Proceeds	125,000
Selling costs (1% × £125,000)	(1,250)
Less: part disposal £70,000 × (125,000/(125,000 + 375,000))	(17,500)
Chargeable gain	106,250

Task 8

Share pool

	No of shares	Cost £
14.4.03 Acquisition	6,000	18,400
29.5.08 Rights 1 for 20 × £4 (1/20 × 6,000)	300	1,200
	6,300	19,600
23.2.26 Disposal (3,500/6,300 × £19,600)	(3,500)	(10,889)
c/f	2,800	8,711

Total gain on sale

	£
First match with acquisitions in the next 30 days:	
Proceeds of sale 500/4,000 × £36,200	4,525
Less allowable cost	(3,400)
Gain	1,125
Next match with shares in the share pool:	
Proceeds of sale 3,500/4,000 × £36,200	31,675
Less allowable cost (from share pool above)	(10,889)
Gain	20,786
Total gains (£1,125 + £20,786)	21,911

Task 9

(a)

Explanation	Exempt (dates)	Chargeable (dates)
Actual occupation	1 April 2009 to 30 September 2012	
Four years employed elsewhere in UK	1 October 2012 to 30 September 2016	
Up to three years any reason	1 October 2016 to 30 September 2017	
Actual occupation	1 October 2017 to 30 April 2018	
Not occupied and not followed by actual occupation		1 May 2018 to 31 December 2024
Last nine months ownership	1 January 2025 to 30 September 2025	

(b) (i) £ 4,000

The capital loss brought forward will be used after the annual exempt amount. This uses £15,000 of the loss, leaving £4,000 to carry forward to 2026/27. (£18,000 – £3,000 – £15,000)

(ii) Jai's taxable gain for 2025/26 is:

£ 10,000

The CGT payable for 2025/26 is:

£ 2,334

	£
Gains	14,000
Less annual exempt amount	(3,000)
Less loss b/f	(1,000)
Taxable gains	10,000
CGT	
£1,110 (W) × 18%	200
£8,890 × 24%	2,134
CGT	2,334

(W) Unused basic rate band is £37,700 + £500 (£400 × 100/80) – £37,090 = £1,110

Task 10

(a) The correct answers are:

	True ✓	False ✓
The taper relief for an individual who survives four but not five years from the date of the gift is 40%.	✓	
Where lifetime tax is paid on CLTs by the donor it is calculated at 20%. **Explanation:** (25%)		✓
Marriage exemptions are only available where the gift is made to relatives. **Explanation:** (£1,000 for any gift)		✓
The annual exemption for the year of the death may be deducted from the death estate. **Explanation:** (AE only available on lifetime transfers)		✓
The residence nil rate band is not available on lifetime transfers.	✓	

(b) **(i)** The correct answer is:

	✓
£55,000	✓
£4,000	
£6,000	
£1,000	

	£
Before the gift: 5,100 shares × £30	153,000
After the gift: 4,900 shares × £20	(98,000)
Diminution in value	55,000

The answer £4,000 is 200 shares at £20. The answer £6,000 is 200 shares at £30. The answer £1,000 is 200 shares at £5.

(ii) The correct answer is:

	✓
£3,000	
£8,500	✓
£6,000	
£11,000	

	£
Marriage exemption (remoter ancestor)	2,500
Annual exemption 2025/26	3,000
Annual exemption 2024/25 b/f	3,000
	8,500

The answer £3,000 is the annual exemption for 2025/26 only. The answer £6,000 ignores the marriage exemption. The answer £11,000 uses the marriage exemption for immediate children.

(iii) The correct answer is:

	✓
£520,000	
£351,000	✓
£350,000	
£1,000	

	£
Cash to nephews £200 × 5	1,000
ISA investments	350,000
Chargeable estate	351,000

The answer £520,000 ignores the spouse exemption. The answer £350,000 forgets the small gifts exemption only applies to lifetime transfers. The answer £1,000 treats the ISA investments as exempt; this exemption only applies for income tax and capital gains tax.

(c)

Gift	Date	Status
Cash to the Conservative political party of £3,000	1 October 2025	Exempt
Shares to her daughter worth £2,700	26 February 2026	Exempt

Gifts to political parties are always exempt. The gift of shares to her daughter is covered by the annual exemption.

Tax Reference material FA 2025

Contents

1 Foreword

This document comprises data that you may need to consult during your Personal Tax computer-based assessment.

The material can be consulted during the practice and live assessments **by using the reference material section at each task position**. It is made available here so you can familiarise yourself with the content before the assessment.

Do not take a print of this document into the exam room with you*.

This document may be changed to reflect periodical updates in the computer-based assessment, so please check you have the most recent version while studying.

This version is based on **Finance Act 2025** and is for use in AAT assessments from **26 January 2026**.

*Unless you need a printed version as part of reasonable adjustments for particular needs, in which case you must discuss this with your tutor at least six weeks before the assessment date.

Professional Conduct in Relation to Taxation (PCRT) sets out the Fundamental Principles and Standards for Tax Planning all members are expected to follow.

Tax advisers operate in a complex business and financial environment and a core purpose of the tax system is to fund public services and to ensure the good health of our economy and society. Tax advisers therefore have a responsibility to serve their clients' interests whilst upholding the profession's reputation and the need to take account of the wider public interest.

PCRT is intended to guide members in their behaviour, to assist them and to ensure that they undertake work effectively and appropriately. If concerns are raised about members, we will take account of these Principles and Standards when deciding whether or not to take action and a failure to comply with PCRT could put members at risk.

Purpose of the Principles and Standards

PCRT describes behaviour required of members, consisting of five Principles and five Standards. There are accompanying Help Sheets which are intended to help members understand and be able to meet the Principles and Standards and provide guidance on issues which are not covered by legislation.

This document has a range of stakeholders covering members, clients, the professional bodies, the public and agencies including the relevant revenue authorities.

We acknowledge that members, students, and those affiliated with the professional bodies work in different environments, both in the UK and overseas, and PCRT has been developed to apply to a wide variety of work settings. PCRT applies to all members providing advice on UK tax matters regardless of contracts of employment, membership of other professional organisations or where in the world they work and reside.

If we are notified of concerns about a member's behaviour involving tax matters, we will take PCRT into consideration to determine whether disciplinary action is required and whether the member continues to uphold the high standards required for membership with our organisations. Members are professionals, able to make informed decisions relating to their work and therefore PCRT is designed to support this.

Tax evasion. A member must never be knowingly involved in tax evasion, although, of course, it is appropriate to act for a client who is rectifying their affairs.

Development of this document

PCRT has been jointly produced by:

- Association of Accounting Technicians (AAT)
- Association of Chartered Certified Accountants (ACCA)
- Association of Taxation Technicians (ATT)
- Chartered Institute of Taxation (CIOT)
- Institute of Chartered Accountants in England and Wales (ICAEW)
- Institute of Chartered Accountants of Scotland (ICAS)
- Society of Trust and Estate Practitioners (STEP)

PCRT has evolved since its introduction in 1995 to take account of changing practices. Additionally, PCRT should be used alongside each organisation's existing Codes of Practice/Conduct, taking into account good practice guidance. HMRC have reflected some of the contents of PCRT into their own **Standards for Agents** (published 4 January 2018).

(While every care has been taken in the preparation of this guidance, the PCRT Bodies do not undertake a duty of care or otherwise for any loss or damage occasioned by reliance on this guidance. Practical guidance cannot and should not be taken to substitute appropriate legal advice).

2 Introduction

2.1 The purpose of Professional Conduct in Relation to Taxation (PCRT) and its associated Help Sheets is to assist and advise members on their professional conduct in relation to taxation, and particularly in the tripartite relationship between a member, client, and the relevant revenue authority. References throughout PCRT to 'relevant revenue authority' are to HMRC, Revenue Scotland or the Welsh Revenue Authority as appropriate. The PCRT consists of the Fundamental Principles and the Standards for Tax Planning.

2.2 Members have a responsibility to attain and thereafter always adhere to the Fundamental Principles and the Standards for Tax Planning in PCRT. If a member fails to do so, they are liable to be subject to disciplinary process.

2.3 The issues addressed in the Help Sheets provide guidance on the application of the PCRT Fundamental Principles and Standards for Tax Planning when dealing with day-to-day work, but they are not intended to be, nor should they be interpreted as, an exhaustive list of all circumstances experienced by a member which may pose threats to compliance with the Fundamental Principles and Standards. Consequently, members must consider and observe the PCRT Fundamental Principles and Standards across all their professional activities.

2.4 If in doubt about the ethical or legal considerations of a particular case, a member should seek advice from their professional body and, where appropriate, their legal advisers. The professional bodies take no responsibility for a member's failure to seek advice where appropriate.

2.5 A member must always fulfil their obligations under the Anti-Money laundering (AML) legislation. AML issues are not covered in detail in the PCRT; the member is instead referred to the Treasury approved **CCAB Anti-Money Laundering and Counter-Terrorist Financing Guidance for the Accountancy Sector (AMLGAS)** (which includes **Supplementary Anti-Money Laundering Guidance for Tax Practitioners**). A member working outside the tax and accountancy sector should refer to the relevant AML guidance for their sector or take advice as appropriate.

2.6 Nothing in PCRT overrides legal professional privilege. Similarly, nothing in PCRT shall override a member's professional duties or be interpreted so as to give rise to any conflict under general law, statutory regulation, or professional regulation of solicitors or barristers, and in the event of any conflict under general law, statutory regulation or such professional regulation shall prevail. For these purposes a conflict shall be considered to arise at least where such law, statutory or such professional regulation to which members are subject would prevent compliance with what would otherwise be required by PCRT.

Application to all members

2.7 While the content of the PCRT is primarily applicable to members in professional practice, the Fundamental Principles and Standards apply to all members who practise in tax including:

- Employees attending to the tax affairs of their employer or of a client; and
- Those dealing with the tax affairs of themselves or others such as family, friends, charities etc. whether or not for payment; and
- Those working in a relevant revenue authority or other public sector bodies or government departments.

2.8 Where a member's employer is not prepared to follow the Fundamental Principles and Standards and/or the ethical approach set out in the Help Sheets (despite the member's reasonable attempts to persuade them to do so) the member may contact their professional body and/or seek legal advice.

2.9 A member who is based overseas or who is acting for a client who is subject to the tax jurisdiction of another country could be subject to more onerous legal obligations under the tax law and/or general law of that country. Except in that situation, a member must apply the Fundamental Principles and Standards to professional activities with non-UK aspects.

2.10 HMRC acknowledges that PCRT is an acceptable basis for dealings between members and HMRC.

Status

2.11 The PCRT has been prepared jointly by the:

- Association of Accounting Technicians
- Association of Chartered Certified Accountants
- Association of Taxation Technicians
- Chartered Institute of Taxation
- Institute of Chartered Accountants in England and Wales
- Institute of Chartered Accountants of Scotland
- Society of Trust and Estate Practitioners

2.12 While every care has been taken in the preparation of PCRT, to the fullest extent permitted by law the author bodies do not accept or assume responsibility to any person or persons who suffer loss or damage occasioned by reliance on PCRT.

Interpretation

2.13 In PCRT:

- Client' includes, where the context requires, 'former client'.
- Member' (and 'members') includes 'firm' or 'practice' and the staff thereof.
- Words in the singular include the plural and words in the plural include the singular.

Abbreviations

2.14 In PCRT the following abbreviations have been used:

AML	Anti-Money Laundering
AMLGAS	AML and Counter-Terrorist Financing Guidance for the Accountancy Sector
CCAB	Consultative Committee of Accountancy Bodies
DOTAS	Disclosure of Tax Avoidance Schemes
DASVOIT	Disclosure of VAT Avoidance Schemes: VAT and Other Indirect Taxes rules
GAAP	Generally Accepted Accounting Principles
GAAR	General Anti-Abuse Rule in Finance Act 2013
GDPR	General Data Protection Regulation
HMRC	HM Revenue and Customs
MTD	Making Tax Digital
MLRO	Money Laundering Reporting Officer

NCA	National Crime Agency
POTAS	Promoters of Tax Avoidance Schemes
PCRT	Professional Conduct in Relation to Taxation
SRN	Scheme Reference Number

3 The Fundamental Principals

3.1 Ethical behaviour in the tax profession is critical. The work carried out by a member needs to be trusted by society at large as well as by clients and other stakeholders. What a member does reflects not just on themselves but on the profession as a whole.

3.2 A member must comply with the following Fundamental Principles.

- **Integrity.** To be straightforward and honest in all professional and business relationships
- **Objectivity.** To not allow bias, conflict of interest or undue influence of others to override professional or business judgements.
- **Professional competence and due care.** To maintain professional knowledge and skill at the level required to ensure that a client or employer receives competent professional service based on current developments in practice, legislation and techniques and act diligently and in accordance with applicable technical and professional standards.
- **Confidentiality.** To respect the confidentiality of information acquired as a result of professional and business relationships and therefore, not disclose any such information to third parties without proper and specific authority, unless there is a legal or professional right or duty to disclose, nor use the information for the personal advantage of the member or third parties.
- **Professional behaviour.** To comply with relevant laws and regulations and avoid any action that discredits the profession.

3.3 Each of these Fundamental Principles is discussed in more detail below in the context of taxation services.

Integrity

3.4 A member must act honestly in all their dealings with their clients, all tax authorities, and other interested parties, and do nothing knowingly or carelessly that might mislead either by commission or omission.

Objectivity

3.5 A member may be exposed to situations that could impair their objectivity. It is impracticable to define and prescribe all such situations. Relationships where there are conflicts of interest or which bias or unduly influence the professional judgement of the member must be avoided.

3.6 A member must explain to their client the material risks of the tax planning or tax positions and the basis on which the advice is given.

3.7 A member must always disclose to their client if they are receiving commission, incentives or any other advantage and the amounts (or the basis on which the amount is calculated) they receive from a third party relating to the matter upon which they are advising their client. They must also follow their professional body's rules on disclosure of and accounting for commission.

Professional competence and due care

3.8 A member has a professional duty to carry out their work within the scope of their engagement and with the requisite skill and care. A member should take care not to stray beyond the agreed terms of the engagement. If they do exceed the scope, they should agree revised terms with their client and check that their professional indemnity insurance covers the enhanced work.

3.9 A member is free to choose whether or not to act for a client both generally and as regards specific activities. However, where a member chooses to limit or amend the scope of services, they provide to a client they should make this clear in writing.

3.10 When advising a client, a member has a duty to serve that client's interests within the relevant legal and regulatory framework.

3.11 A member must carry out their work with a proper regard for the technical and professional standards expected. A member must not undertake professional work which they are not competent to perform unless they obtain appropriate assistance from a suitably qualified specialist.

3.12 A member who is giving what they believe to be a significant opinion to a client should consider obtaining a second opinion to support the advice. Where the second opinion is to be obtained externally, due regard must be had to client confidentiality.

3.13 Advice should be given in the context of the commercial and other non-tax objectives and the facts and circumstances of the client.

3.14 On occasions there may be more than one tenable interpretation of the law. Each case should be considered on its own individual facts and circumstances.

Confidentiality

3.15 Confidentiality is a professional principle and is also a legally enforceable contractual obligation. It may be an express term of the engagement letter between the member and the client. Where it is not an express term, a court would in most circumstances treat confidentiality as an implied contractual term.

3.16 A member may only disclose information without their client's consent when there is an express legal or professional right or duty to disclose.

3.17 The duty of confidentiality is rigorously safeguarded by the courts. Disclosure of confidential material in a member's own interest must be made only where it is considered adequate, relevant, and reasonably necessary for the administration of justice - in other words, when a member reasonably considers that it would otherwise impair the pursuit of their legitimate interests and rights if they were prevented from disclosing the information in all the circumstances. Only the minimum amount of information necessary to protect those interests may be disclosed. Examples of such circumstances may include, but are not limited to, the following:

- To enable a member to defend themself against a criminal charge or to clear themself of suspicion.
- To enable a member to defend themself in disciplinary proceedings
- To resist proceedings for a penalty, or civil or criminal proceedings in respect of a taxation offence, for example in a case where it is suggested that a member knowingly engaged in dishonest conduct with a view to bringing about a loss of tax revenue.
- To resist a legal action made against them by a client or third party.
- To enable a member to sue for unpaid fees.
- To enable a member to sue for defamation.

3.18 If there is any doubt that the circumstances in 3.17 would apply, or there is the risk of challenge by a client or employer, a member is strongly recommended to seek legal advice. See also the Help Sheet on **Dealing with Errors.**

3.19 The Anti-Money laundering regime provides a statutory code to determine when a disclosure must be made to NCA. While this is a mandatory regime, it also gives a structure for the assessment of the public interest in a tax context, including which of the following should take precedence, in a particular set of circumstances:

- The public interest in reporting knowledge or suspicions of criminal activity to the authorities; or
- The public interest in clients receiving advice in confidence.

3.20 A member should follow the Treasury approved **CCAB AMLGAS** and the Treasury approved **Supplementary Anti-Money Laundering Guidance for Tax Practitioners.** See also the Help Sheet **Request for data by HMRC.**

Professional behaviour

3.21 A member must always act in a way that will not bring them or their professional body into disrepute.

3.22 A member must behave with courtesy and consideration towards all with whom they come into contact in a professional capacity.

3.23 A member must comply with all relevant legal and regulatory obligations when dealing with a client's tax affairs and assist their clients to do the same. A member who has reason to believe that proposed arrangements are, or may be, tax evasion must strongly advise clients not to enter into them. If a client chooses to ignore that advice, it is difficult to envisage situations where it would be appropriate for a member to continue to act other than in rectifying the client's affairs.

3.24 Serving the interests of their clients will, on occasion, bring a member into disagreement or conflict with a relevant revenue authority. A member should manage such disagreements or conflicts in an open, constructive, and professional manner. However, a member should serve their clients' interests as robustly as circumstances warrant whilst applying these principles.

3.25 A member should consider whether any tax arrangements with which they might be associated on their own behalf or on behalf of a client might bring the member and the profession into disrepute. In this regard, members are referred to the Standards for Tax Planning set out in para 4.9 below (see also the Help Sheet on **Tax Advice** for more detail).

3.26 A member's own tax affairs should be kept up to date. Neglect of a member's own affairs could raise doubts within a relevant revenue authority as to the standard of the member's professional work and could bring them or their professional body into disrepute.

3.27 A member should ensure that their internal and external communications including those using social media are consistent with the principles in this guidance and in particular confidentiality.

4 The Standards for Tax Planning

4.1 In order to protect the reputation of members, the wider profession, and ensure that public interest concerns are met, the PCRT bodies have developed further Standards that members must observe when advising on UK tax planning. These seek to build on the Fundamental Principles set out above, focusing in particular on integrity, professional competence, and behaviour. The Standards are a supplement to, and not a substitute for, the five Fundamental Principles. These standards have been developed in the specific context of the UK including the role of the legislature in making tax law, of the relevant revenue authorities in administering it, and the courts and tribunals in enforcing it.

4.2 The Standards are set out below:

Client Specific

Tax planning must be specific to the client's facts and circumstances. Clients must be alerted to the wider risks and the implications of any courses of action.

Lawful

At all times members must act lawfully and with integrity and expect the same from their clients. Tax planning should be based on a realistic assessment of the facts and on a credible view of the law. Members should draw their clients' attention to where the law is materially uncertain, for example because the relevant revenue authority is known to take a different view of the law. Members should consider taking further advice appropriate to the risks and circumstances of the particular case, for example where litigation is likely.

Disclosure and transparency

Tax advice must not rely for its effectiveness on the relevant revenue authority having less than the relevant facts. Any disclosure must fairly represent all relevant facts.

Advising on tax planning arrangements

Members must not create, encourage, or promote tax planning arrangements or structures that: i) set out to achieve results that are contrary to the clear intention of Parliament in enacting relevant legislation; and/or ii) are highly artificial or highly contrived and seek to exploit shortcomings within the relevant legislation.

Professional judgement and appropriate documentation

Applying these requirements to particular client advisory situations requires members to exercise professional judgement on a number of matters. Members should keep notes on a timely basis of the rationale for the judgments exercised in seeking to adhere to these requirements.

Further discussion on the Standards is set out below:

Client Specific

4.3 The risks referred to in this Standard are those which are directly attributable to the planning and could be reasonably foreseeable by the member. There would not normally be a duty to comment on, for example, the commercial risk of the underlying transaction. The obligations of the member to the client continue to be governed by the engagement letter.

4.4 Where wider risks should be highlighted, the member may either advise on them, or identify them as matters on which separate advice should be sought by the client, depending on the scope of the member's practice and of the engagement.

4.5 Generic opinions or advice that does not take into account the position of specific taxpayers (or a narrowly defined group of taxpayers such as a group of employees of the same company) pose particular risks. Members are entitled to make reasonable assumptions in giving advice (for example, where it would be reasonable on the facts to assume that the taxpayer(s) is/are UK resident), but assumptions should not be relied upon which are known to be unrealistic or unreasonable. If advice is generic, and/or depends on certain assumptions, this fact, and the need for specific advice to be taken before acting should be highlighted with sufficient prominence to prevent any misunderstandings arising*. Members should consider including in their advice the potential impact of a change in the assumptions made and/or the circumstances which might require specific or updated advice to be obtained.

**For some suitably qualified members, this might, for example, include the preparation of standard wording for inclusion in contracts, wills or other documents.*

Lawful

4.6 The requirement to advise clients on material uncertainty in the law (including where the relevant revenue authority is known to take a different view) applies even if the practical likelihood of intervention by the authority is considered low. Clients should be told what would be reasonable, at the time of the transaction, to expect the authority to believe the application of the law to be (assuming the authority was fully appraised of all the facts of the transaction). Where the likely view of the authority is uncertain or not known, the member should include this fact as part of their advice.

4.7 The fact that the member may disagree with the relevant authority on a matter is not of itself indicative of behaviour that might breach these standards. A member may reasonably believe that an authority's view is wrong in law but, if so, the client should be alerted to the fact that the authority holds a different view of the law and should be advised of the risks and likely costs that might be incurred in order to determine any dispute.

Disclosure and transparency

4.8 Disclosure should be made whenever required by law and fuller disclosure must be recommended to clients wherever it is appropriate given a wider relationship or dialogue with the relevant revenue authority that is relevant to that client. What is actually to be disclosed will inevitably reflect a professional judgement taking into account all relevant facts and law specific to the case in question and what the client consents should be disclosed.

Tax planning arrangements

4.9 Where a member has a genuine and reasonable uncertainty as to whether particular planning is in breach of this standard, the member should:

- document the detailed reasoning and evidence sufficiently to be able to demonstrate why they took the view that any planning was not in breach of this standard.
- include in their client advice an assessment of uncertainties and risks involved in the planning - see Standard Lawful above.
- include in their client advice an assessment of the relevant disclosures that should be made to the relevant revenue authority to enable it, should it wish to do so, to make any reasonable enquiries – see Standard Disclosure and transparency above.

Professional judgement and appropriate documentation

4.10 Members are not required to complete paperwork for its own sake, but they should be prepared to identify, support and where appropriate defend the judgements they made in applying these requirements to their work.

4.11 Where the judgements made are reasonable, notes taken on a timely basis are likely to be the most convincing way of demonstrating compliance with the principles after the event, to the benefit of the member and the client and to satisfy any wider public concerns.

5 PCRT Help sheet A: Submission of tax information and 'tax filings'

This help sheet provides guidance on the application of the ***PCRT Fundamental Principles and Standards for Tax Planning*** *when dealing with the day-to-day work of filing tax information and completing tax filings, including the issues of responsibilities, materiality, disclosure and approval. If appropriate, please also refer to* ***Help sheet B on Tax Advice***.

Definition of filing of tax information and tax filings (filing)

5.1 For the purposes of this guidance, the term 'filing' includes any online submission of data, online filing or other filing that is prepared on behalf of the client for the purposes of disclosing to any taxing authority details that are to be used in the calculation of tax due by a client or a refund of tax due to the client or for other official purposes. It includes all taxes, NIC and duties.

5.2 A letter, or online notification, giving details in respect of a filing or as an amendment to a filing including, for example, any voluntary disclosure of an error should be dealt with as if it was a filing.

Making Tax Digital and filing

5.3 Tax administration systems, including the UK's, are increasingly moving to mandatory digital filing of tax information and returns.

5.4 Except in exceptional circumstances, a member will explicitly file in their capacity as agent. A member is advised to use the facilities provided for agents and to avoid knowing or using the client's personal access credentials.

5.5 A member should keep their access credentials safe from unauthorised use and consider periodic change of passwords.

5.6 A member is recommended to forward suspicious emails to **phishing@hmrc.gsi.gov.uk** and then delete them. It is also important to avoid clicking on websites or links in suspicious emails, or opening attachments.

5.7 Firms should have policies on cyber security, AML and GDPR.

Taxpayer's responsibility

5.8 The taxpayer has primary responsibility to submit correct and complete filings to the best of their knowledge and belief. The final decision as to whether to disclose any issue is that of the client but in relation to your responsibilities see paragraph 12 below.

5.9 In annual self-assessment returns or returns with short filing periods the filing may include reasonable estimates where necessary.

Member's responsibility

5.10 A member who prepares a filing on behalf of a client is responsible to the client for the accuracy of the filing based on the information provided.

5.11 In dealing with HMRC in relation to a client's tax affairs a member should bear in mind their duty of confidentiality to the client and that they are acting as the agent of their client. They have a duty to act in the best interests of their client.

5.12 A member should act in good faith in dealings with HMRC in accordance with the fundamental principle of **integrity.** In particular the member should take reasonable care and exercise appropriate professional scepticism when making statements or asserting facts on behalf of a client.

5.13 Where acting as a tax agent, a member is not required to audit the figures in the books and records provided or verify information provided by a client or by a third party. However, a member should take care not to be associated with the presentation of facts they know or believe to be incorrect or misleading, not to assert tax positions in a tax filing which they consider to have no sustainable basis.

5.14 When a member is communicating with HMRC, they should consider whether they need to make it clear to what extent they are relying on information which has been supplied by the client or a third party.

Materiality

5.15 Whether an amount is to be regarded as material depends upon the facts and circumstances of each case.

5.16 The profits of a trade, profession, vocation or property business should be computed in accordance with GAAP subject to any adjustment required or authorised by law in computing profits for those purposes. This permits a trade, profession, vocation or property business to disregard non-material adjustments in computing its accounting profits.

5.17 The application of GAAP, and therefore materiality does not extend beyond the accounting profits. Thus, the accounting concept of materiality cannot be applied when completing tax filings.

5.18 It should be noted that for certain small businesses an election may be made to use the cash basis instead; for small property businesses the default position is the cash basis. Where the cash basis is used, materiality is not relevant.

Disclosure

5.19 If a client is unwilling to include in a tax filing the minimum information required by law, the member should follow the guidance in **Help sheet C: Dealing with Errors**. The paragraphs below (paras 20 – 24) give guidance on some of the more common areas of uncertainty over disclosure.

5.20 In general, it is likely to be in a client's own interests to ensure that factors relevant to their tax liability are adequately disclosed to HMRC because:

- their relationship with HMRC is more likely to be on a satisfactory footing if they can demonstrate good faith in their dealings with them. HMRC notes in 'Your Charter' that 'We want to give you a service that is fair, accurate and based on mutual trust and respect', and
- they will reduce the risk of a discovery or further assessment and may reduce exposure to interest and penalties.

5.21 It may be advisable to consider fuller disclosure than is strictly necessary. Reference to **'The Standards for Tax Planning'** in **PCRT** may be relevant. The factors involved in making this decision include:

- a filing relies on a valuation
- the terms of the applicable law
- the view taken by the member
- the extent of any doubt that exists
- the manner in which disclosure is to be made
- the size and gravity of the item in question.

5.22 When advocating fuller disclosure than is necessary a member should ensure that their client is adequately aware of the issues involved and their potential implications. Fuller disclosure should only be made with the client's consent.

5.23 Cases will arise where there is doubt as to the correct treatment of an item of income or expenditure, or the computation of a gain or allowance. In such cases a member ought to consider what additional disclosure, if any, might be necessary. For example, additional disclosure should be considered where:

- there is inherent doubt as to the correct treatment of an item, for example, expenditure on repairs which might be regarded as capital in whole or part, or the VAT liability of a particular transaction, or
- HMRC has published its interpretation or has indicated its practice on a point, but the client proposes to adopt a different view, whether or not supported by Counsel's opinion. The member should refer to the guidance on the **Veltema case** and the paragraph below. See also **HMRC guidance.**

5.24 A member who is uncertain whether their client should disclose a particular item or of its treatment should consider taking further advice before reaching a decision. They should use their best endeavours to ensure that the client understands the issues, implications and the proposed course of action. Such a decision may have to be justified at a later date, so the member's files should contain sufficient evidence to support the position taken, including timely notes of discussions with the client and/or with other advisors, copies of any second opinion obtained and the client's final decision. A failure to take reasonable care may result in HMRC imposing a penalty if an error is identified after an enquiry.

Supporting documents

5.25 For the most part, HMRC does not consider that it is necessary for a taxpayer to provide supporting documentation in order to satisfy the taxpayer's overriding need to make a correct filing. HMRC's view is that, where it is necessary for that purpose, explanatory information should be entered in the 'white space' provided on the filing. However, HMRC does recognise that the taxpayer may wish to supply further details of a particular computation or transaction in order to minimise the risk of a discovery assessment being raised at a later time. Following the uncertainty created by the decision in Veltema, HMRC's guidance can be found in **SP1/06 – Self Assessment: Finality and Discovery.**

5.26 Further HMRC guidance says that sending attachments with a tax filing is intended for those cases where the taxpayer 'feels it is crucial to provide additional information to support the filing but for some reason cannot utilise the white space'.

Reliance on HMRC published guidance

5.27 Whilst it is reasonable in most circumstances to rely on HMRC published guidance, a member should be aware that the Tribunal and the courts will apply the law even if this conflicts with HMRC guidance.

5.28 Notwithstanding this, if a client has relied on HMRC guidance which is clear and unequivocal and HMRC resiles from any of the terms of the guidance, a Judicial Review claim is a possible route to pursue.

Approval of tax filings

5.29 The member should advise the client to review their tax filing before it is submitted.

5.30 The member should draw the client's attention to the responsibility which the client is taking in approving the filing as correct and complete. Attention should be drawn to any judgmental areas or positions reflected in the filing to ensure that the client is aware of these and their implications before they approve the filing.

5.31 A member should obtain evidence of the client's approval of the filing in electronic or non-electronic form.

Exceptions

5.32 Where a filing is not reviewed by the client before submission, then, because of the risk to the adviser, the terms of the engagement should make clear that filings are completed on the basis of the information provided by the client and the client is no less responsible for errors in filings which have been prepared on the basis of that information than if they had approved and signed the filings personally.

5.33 A member may approve tax filings in their capacity as liquidator, receiver or administrator or under a personal appointment as trustee, executor, attorney or director. If a member is approving a tax return on behalf of a client, the member should carefully consider:

- Their legal authority to do so (for example, is a power of attorney required);
- The process whereby the client will review and take responsibility for the contents of the return; and
- Any legal implications of approving the return for both the practice and the individual signatory.

Referrals/ Second opinions

5.34 A member needs to be mindful of the Code of Ethics requirement regarding **professional competence**. For example, a member who generally advises on annual tax compliance but receives a request from a client regarding IHT planning should consider whether they have the relevant skills and knowledge to properly service the client on that matter. If not, the member should refer the client to another member who is a specialist in this area. (See Mehjoo v Harben Barker 2014 EWCA Civ 358).

5.35 Where a second opinion is sought on any tax advice, it should be from a suitably qualified and experienced professional who is subject to the requirements of PCRT or its equivalent.

Support

5.36 A member may wish to put in place arrangements with another firm or a member of one of the professional bodies to be able to seek support when necessary and to ensure that there would be a minimum of disruption, in the event of the incapacity or death of the sole practitioner.

Alternates

5.37 Note that it is a requirement of the Client Money Regulations, should the member hold client monies, to have an alternate to ensure that there would be a minimum of disruption, in the event of the incapacity or death of the sole practitioner.

Third party advice involving tax planning arrangements

5.38 If a member, acting in their capacity as an agent submitting a tax filing on behalf of a client, is asked by the client to include in their tax return specific items of tax planning based on third party advice, the member may have concerns. The member should satisfy themselves that such third-party advice is reasonable by considering:

- Does it accord with their understanding of the law?
- Is the person giving the advice appropriately qualified and a member of a PCRT body or an equivalent regime?

5.39 For more complex planning, and with the **PCRT Standards for Tax Planning** in mind, the member should consider:

- Do the background facts set out in the advice agree with their understanding of the client?
- Do any legal opinions in the advice relate specifically to the advice?
- Is the advice current?
- Does the tax planning provided by the third party appear to involve contrived avoidance?
- If so, does this look like a spotlighted scheme?
- Might this scheme be caught by the General Anti-abuse Rule (GAAR) or the Scottish General Anti-Avoidance Rule (SGAAR)?
- If the member has concerns about the third party advice, is it so significant that the member needs a second opinion rather than caveating their compliance responsibility

These points are discussed further in **Help sheet B: Tax Advice.**

While every care has been taken in the preparation of this guidance the PCRT Bodies do not undertake a duty of care or otherwise for any loss or damage occasioned by reliance on this guidance. Practical guidance cannot and should not be taken to substitute appropriate legal advice.

6 PCRT Help sheet B: Tax advice

This help sheet provides guidance on the application of the ***PCRT Fundamental Principles and Standards for Tax Planning.*** *This help sheet includes the Standards for Tax Planning, further discussion of the Standards, and FAQs which are designed to illustrate the practical application of the Standards.*

The Standards for Tax Planning

6.1 The Standards for Tax Planning are critical to any planning undertaken by members.

They are:

- **Client Specific**

  Tax planning must be specific to the particular client's facts and circumstances. Clients must be alerted to the wider risks and implications of any courses of action.

- **Lawful**

  At all times members must act lawfully and with integrity and expect the same from their clients. Tax planning should be based on a realistic assessment of the facts and on a credible view of the law.

  Members should draw their client's attention to where the law is materially uncertain, for example because HMRC is known to take a different view of the law. Members should consider taking further advice appropriate to the risks and circumstances of the particular case, for example where litigation is likely.

- **Disclosure and transparency**

  Tax advice must not rely for its effectiveness on HMRC having less than the relevant facts. Any disclosure must fairly represent all relevant facts.

- **Tax planning arrangements**

  Members must not create, encourage or promote tax planning arrangements or structures that i) set out to achieve results that are contrary to the clear intention of Parliament in enacting relevant legislation and/or ii) are highly artificial or highly contrived and seek to exploit shortcomings within the relevant legislation.

- **Professional judgement and appropriate documentation**

Applying these requirements to particular client advisory situations requires members to exercise professional judgement on a number of matters. Members should keep notes on a timely basis of the rationale for the judgements exercised in seeking to adhere to these requirements.

6.2 Further discussion on these Standards for Tax Planning is set out below:

Client Specific

6.3 The risks referred to in this Standard are those which are directly attributable to the planning and could be reasonably foreseeable by the member. There would not normally be a duty to comment on, for example, the commercial risk of the underlying transaction. The obligations of the member to the client continue to be governed by the engagement letter.

6.4 Where wider risks should be highlighted, the member may either advise on them, or identify them as matters on which separate advice should be sought by the client, depending on the scope of the member's practice and of the engagement.

6.5 Generic opinions or advice that does not consider the position of specific taxpayers (or a narrowly defined group of taxpayers such as a group of employees of the same company) pose risks. Members are entitled to make reasonable assumptions in giving advice (for example, where it would be reasonable on the facts to assume that the taxpayer(s) is/are UK resident), but assumptions should not be relied upon which are known to be unrealistic or unreasonable. If advice is generic, and/or depends on certain assumptions, this fact, and the need for specific advice to be taken before acting should be highlighted with sufficient prominence to prevent any misunderstandings arising*. Members should consider including in their advice the potential impact of a change in the assumptions made and/or the circumstances which might require specific or updated advice to be obtained.

**For some suitably qualified members, this might, for example, include the preparation of standard wording for inclusion in contracts, Wills or other documents.*

Lawful

6.6 The requirement to advise clients on material uncertainty in the law (including where HMRC take a different view) applies even if the practical likelihood of HMRC intervention is considered low. Clients should be told what would be reasonable, at the time of the transaction, to expect HMRC to believe the application of the law to be (assuming HMRC was fully apprised of all the facts of the transaction). Where the likely view of HMRC is uncertain or not known, the member should include this fact as part of their advice.

6.7 The fact that the member may disagree with HMRC on a matter is not of itself indicative of behaviour that might breach these standards. A member may reasonably believe that an HMRC view is wrong in law but, if so, the client should be alerted to the fact that HMRC holds a different view of the law and should be advised of the risks and likely costs that might be incurred to determine any dispute.

Disclosure and transparency

6.8 Disclosure should be made whenever required by law and fuller disclosure must be recommended to clients wherever it is appropriate given a wider relationship or dialogue with HMRC relevant to that client. What is to be disclosed will inevitably reflect a professional judgement considering all relevant facts and law specific to the case in question and what the client consents should be disclosed.

Tax planning arrangements

6.9 Where a member has a genuine and reasonable uncertainty as to whether particular planning is in breach of this Standard, the member should:

- document the detailed reasoning and evidence sufficiently to be able to demonstrate why they took the view that any planning was not in breach of this Standard;
- include in their client advice an assessment of uncertainties and risks involved in the planning - see Standard **Lawful** above; and
- include in their client advice an assessment of the relevant disclosures that should be made to HMRC to enable it, should it wish to do so, to make any reasonable enquiries – see Standard **Disclosure and transparency** above.

Professional judgement and appropriate documentation

6.10 Members are not required to complete paperwork for its own sake, but they should be prepared to identify, support and where appropriate defend the judgements they made in applying these requirements to their work.

6.11 Where the judgements made are reasonable, notes taken on a timely basis are likely to be the most convincing way of demonstrating compliance with the principles after the event, to the benefit of the member and the client and to satisfy any wider public concerns.

Guidance

6.12 The paragraphs below provide guidance for members when considering whether advice complies with the Fundamental Principles and Standards for Tax Planning.

Tax evasion

6.13 A member should never be knowingly involved in tax evasion, although, of course, it is appropriate to act for a client who is rectifying their affairs.

Tax planning and advice

6.14 In contrast to tax evasion, tax planning is legal. However, under the Standard members 'must not create, encourage or promote tax planning arrangements that (i) set out to achieve results that are contrary to the clear intention of Parliament in enacting relevant legislation and/or (ii) are highly artificial or highly contrived and seek to exploit shortcomings within the relevant legislation'.

6.15 Things to consider:

- Have you checked that your engagement letter fully covers the scope of the planning advice?
- Have you taken the Standards for Tax Planning and the Fundamental Principles into account? Is it client specific? Is it lawful? Will all relevant facts be disclosed to HMRC? Is it creating, encouraging or promoting tax planning contrary to the 4th Standard for Tax Planning.
- How tax sophisticated is the client?
- Has the client made clear what they wish to achieve by the planning?
- What are the issues involved with the implementation of the planning?
- What are the risks associated with the planning and have you warned the client of them? For example:
    - The strength of the legal interpretation relied upon.
    - The potential application of the GAAR.
    - The implications for the client, including the obligations of the client in relation to their tax return, if the planning requires disclosure under DOTAS or DASVOIT and the potential for an accelerated payment notice or partner payment notice?
    - The reputational risk to the client and the member of the planning in the public arena.
    - The stress, cost and wider personal or business implications to the client in the event of a prolonged dispute with HMRC. This may involve unwelcomed publicity, costs, expenses and loss of management time over a significant period.
    - If the client tenders for government contracts, the potential impact of the proposed tax planning on tendering for and retaining public sector contracts.
    - The risk of counteraction. This may occur before the planning is completed or potentially there may be retrospective counteraction at a later date.
    - The risk of challenge by HMRC. Such challenge may relate to the legal interpretation relied upon, but may alternatively relate to the construction of the facts, including the implementation of the planning.

  - The risk and inherent uncertainty of litigation. The probability of the planning being overturned by the courts if litigated and the potential ultimate downside should the client be unsuccessful.
  - Is a second opinion necessary/advisable?
- Are the arrangements in line with any applicable code of conduct or ethical guidelines or stances for example the Banking Code, and fit and proper tests for charity trustees and pension administrators?
- Are you satisfied that the client understands the planning proposed?
- Have you documented the advice given and the reasoning behind it?

HMRC guidance

6.16 HMRC publications in respect of Tax avoidance and Tax evasion can be found on Gov.uk.

While every care has been taken in the preparation of this guidance the PCRT Bodies do not undertake a duty of care or otherwise for any loss or damage occasioned by reliance on this guidance. Practical guidance cannot and should not be taken to substitute appropriate legal advice.

7 PCRT Help sheet C: Dealing with errors

Introduction

This help sheet provides guidance on the application of the ***PCRT Fundamental Principles and Standards for Tax Planning*** *when dealing with errors that arise in tax. This includes establishing the facts, whether client authorisation is needed to disclose an error and actions to take where a client refuses to disclose.*

Guidance details

7.1 For the purposes of this guidance, the term 'error' is intended to include all errors and mistakes whether they were made by the client, the member, HMRC or any other party involved in a client's tax affairs, and whether made innocently or deliberately.

7.2 During a member's relationship with the client, the member may become aware of possible errors in the client's tax affairs. Unless the client is already aware of the possible error, they should be informed as soon as the member identifies them.

7.3 Where the error has resulted in the client paying too much tax the member should advise the client to make a repayment claim. The member should advise the client of the time limits to make a claim and have regard to any relevant time limits. The rest of this Help sheet deals with situations where tax may be due to HMRC.

7.4 Sometimes an error made by HMRC may mean that the client has not paid tax actually due or they have been incorrectly repaid tax. There may be fee costs as a result of correcting such mistakes. A member should bear in mind that, in some circumstances, clients or agents may be able to claim for additional professional costs incurred and compensation from HMRC. (See **HMRC's complaints factsheet. https://www.gov.uk/complain-about-hmrc**).

7.5 A member should act correctly from the outset. A member should keep sufficient appropriate records of discussions and advice and when dealing with errors the member should:

- give the client appropriate advice;
- if necessary, so long as they continue to act for the client, seek to persuade the client to behave correctly;
- take care not to appear to be assisting a client to plan or commit any criminal offence or to conceal any offence which has been committed; and
- in appropriate situations, or where in doubt, discuss the client's situation with a colleague or an independent third party (having due regard to client confidentiality).

7.6 Once aware of a possible error, a member must bear in mind the legislation on money laundering and the obligations and duties which this places upon them.

7.7 Where the member may have made the error, the member should consider whether they need to notify their professional indemnity insurers.

7.8 In any situation where a member has concerns about their own position, they should consider taking specialist legal advice. For example, where a client appears to have used the member to assist in the commissioning of a criminal offence and people could question whether the member had acted honestly in in good faith. Note that **The Criminal Finances Act 2017** has created new criminal offences of failure to prevent facilitation of tax evasion.

7.9 The flowchart below summarises the recommended steps a member should take where a possible error arises. It must be read in conjunction with the guidance and commentary that follow it.

Dealing with errors flowchart

Dealing with errors flowchart

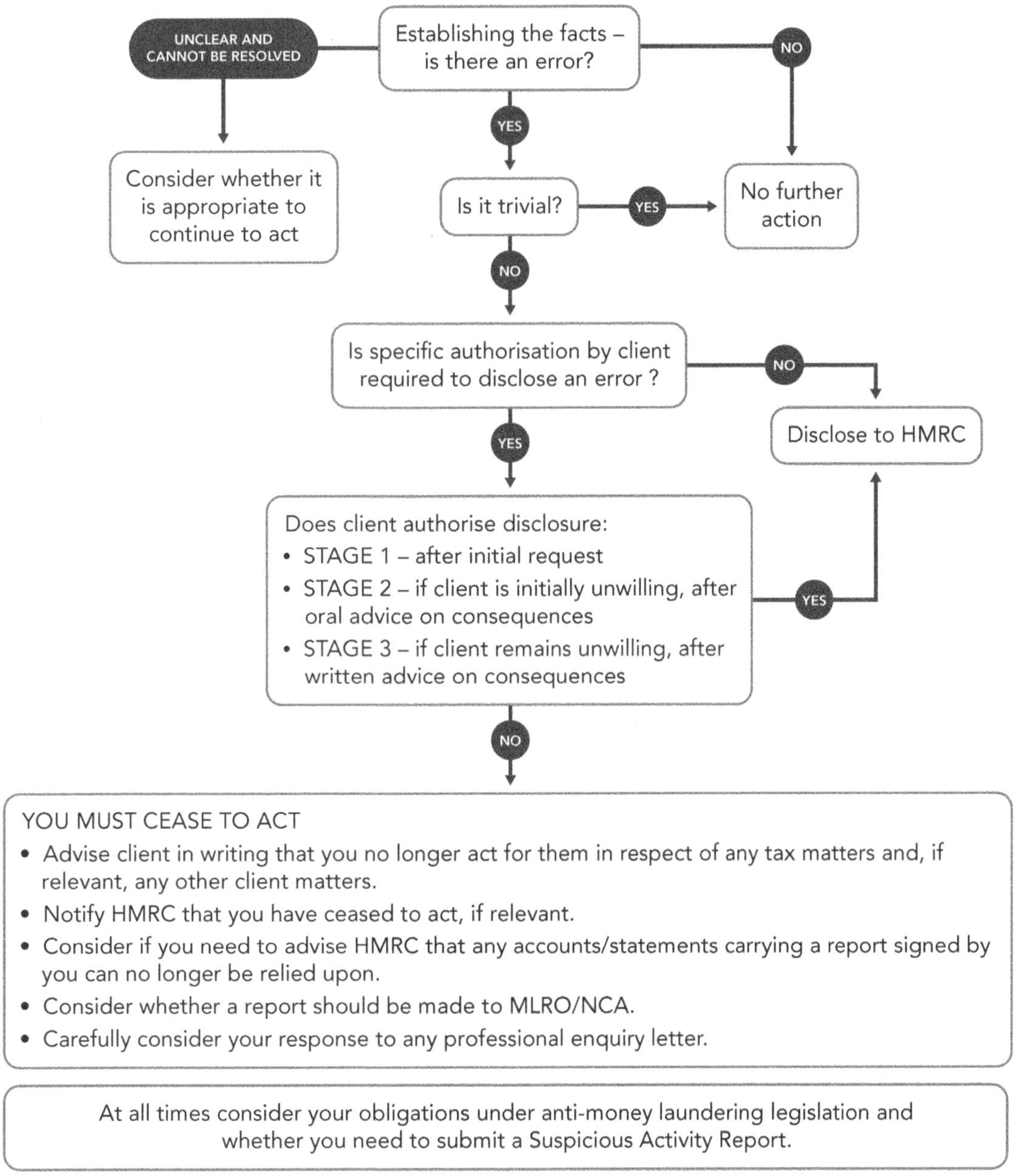

Establishing the facts

7.10 A member is not required to make enquiries to identify errors which are unrelated to the work they have been engaged to perform. However, if they become aware of any error in a client's tax affairs they should follow this guidance, whether or not the error related to a matter they have acted on.

7.11 A member who suspects that an error may have occurred should discuss this with the client to remove or confirm the suspicion. They should take into account the fact that the client may not be aware of all the facts and circumstances and the member may not, therefore, be able to reach a conclusion.

7.12 Where the client provides an explanation for the apparent error to the satisfaction of the member, the member is free to continue to act for that client.

7.13 Where the client fails to explain the apparent error to the satisfaction of the member, the member should consider whether it is appropriate to continue to act. Where the member concludes that it is appropriate to continue to act they should monitor the position carefully. Should it later become apparent that there is an error despite the client's previous assurances to the contrary, the member should follow the advice in the flowchart above. In cases where a member ceases to act, they should follow the guidance below (see sections: Ceasing to act; Informing HMRC)

7.14 Withdrawing reports signed by the member; Reporting to MLRO/NCA and professional enquiry).

7.15 If a member is unsure whether there is an error the member should consider seeking specialist advice. Likewise correcting more serious errors may also require specialist help. In some situations, the client may wish to seek, or advise the client, to seek a second opinion.

7.16 Whether the member decides to continue to act for the client or not, the member should protect their position by documenting:

- The discussions they have had with their client, any colleague, specialist and/or HMRC;
- The client's explanations; and
- Their conclusion and the reasons for reaching that conclusion. It may be appropriate to confirm the facts in writing with the client.

Is the error trivial?

7.17 As a general principle all known errors should be corrected (save for non-material adjustments as described above). In the opinion of the professional bodies it is reasonable for a member to take no steps to advise HMRC of isolated errors where the tax effect is no more than minimal, say up to £200, as these will probably cost HMRC and the client more to process than they are worth to the Exchequer.

Does a member need specific authorisation from the client to disclose an error?

7.18 A member must ensure that they have authority to disclose an error to HMRC.

7.19 This could be specific authority agreed with the client or a general authority contained in a letter of engagement. If in any doubt, or if the amount of tax involved is material, the member should confirm the position with the client.

7.20 If the client withdraws the member's authority to correct the error, the member should follow the guidance below (see sections: Actions where the client refuses to disclose, Ceasing to act, Informing HMRC, Withdrawing reports signed by the member, Reporting to MLRO/NCA and professional enquiry).

7.21 A member must have the client's authority to agree a negotiated figure following disclosure of the facts and circumstances. A member cannot agree a figure that they know to contain an error.

7.22 In all cases where HMRC has sent an over-repayment to the member they must return it to HMRC as soon as practicable. A member does not require their client's authority to return an excessive repayment but, as a matter of course, they should notify their client that they have done so.

Stage 1: Asking the client for authority to disclose

7.23 Subject to the circumstances set out above (see section: Does a member need specific authorisation from the client to disclose an error?), the member should ask the client's permission to notify HMRC of the error. A member should encourage the client to make a timely disclosure. The member should advise the client of their obligations under the relevant tax legislation and refer, as relevant, to interest and penalties for errors.

7.24 Whether the client follows the member's advice is, ultimately, the client's decision. If, however, the client decides not to act in accordance with the member's advice on their obligations, the member should take the further steps detailed below (see sections: Stage 2; Stage 3; Actions where the client refuses to disclose; Ceasing to act; Informing HMRC; Withdrawing reports signed by the member; Reporting to MLRO/NCA and professional enquiry).

Stage 2: Advising the client of the consequences of failure to disclose

7.25 Where it appears that the client is reluctant to authorise disclosure of the error to HMRC, the member should explain to the client:

- The potential consequences of non-disclosure;
- The benefit of making a voluntary disclosure especially as regards reduced penalties; and
- The wide ranging powers to obtain information from taxpayers, their agents and third parties available to HMRC.

7.26 This will also include the member explaining that they will:

- Be required to put their advice that disclosure is required in writing;
- Be obliged to cease to act and in some circumstances to disassociate themself from any work done, should disclosure not be made. The client should be left in no doubt that adverse inferences could be made and that this step could result in HMRC commencing enquiries which might lead to the discovery of the non-disclosure; and
- Comply with their professional obligations relating to the appointment of a new adviser, as it is the duty of professional advisers before accepting professional work to communicate with the person who previously acted in connection with that work.

7.27 Where the client is an organisation and the client contact still remains reluctant to authorise disclosure of the error to HMRC, the member should raise the issue at a higher level within the client organisation. If, having followed this approach, the client continues to be reluctant to authorise disclosure to HMRC, the member should follow the guidance set out below (see sections: Stage 3; Actions where the client refuses to disclose; Ceasing to act; Informing HMRC; Withdrawing reports signed by the member; Reporting to MLRO/NCA and professional enquiry).

Stage 3: Advising the client in writing of the consequences of failure to disclose

7.28 Where the client remains unwilling to make a full disclosure to HMRC the member should ensure that they can show they have acted properly. It is essential to advise the client in writing, setting out the facts as understood by the member, confirming to the client the member's advice to disclose and the consequences of non-disclosure.

7.29 If, after being advised in writing, the client delays making a full disclosure, the member should consider at which point the delay should be treated as a refusal to disclose.

Actions where the client refuses to disclose

7.30 If, despite being fully advised of the consequences, the client still refuses to make an appropriate disclosure to HMRC, the member must:

- Cease to act;
- If relevant, inform HMRC of their withdrawal; and should:
- Consider withdrawing reports signed by the member;
- Consider whether a money laundering report should be made to the firm's MLRO/NCA, and
- Consider carefully their response to any professional enquiry letter (also known as professional clearance letter).

These obligations are set out in more detail below.

Ceasing to act

7.31 Where the member should cease to act in relation to the client's tax affairs they should inform the client of this in writing.

7.32 If HMRC were to realise that the member had continued to act after becoming aware of such undisclosed errors, the member's relationship with HMRC could be damaged. HMRC might, in some circumstances, consider the member to be knowingly or carelessly involved in the commission of an offence or be engaged in dishonest conduct.

7.33 The member should consider carefully whether it is appropriate to continue to act in relation to any non-tax matters of the client.

Informing HMRC

7.34 Where the member had been dealing with HMRC on the client's behalf or had been formally appointed as a tax agent, the member should notify HMRC that they have ceased to act for that client. Because of the obligation to maintain client confidentiality a member should not provide HMRC with an explanation as to the reasons for ceasing to act.

Withdrawing reports signed by the member

7.35 Where a member has undertaken work to verify or audit accounts or statements which carry a report signed by the member and these reports are subsequently found to be misleading, the same principles of client confidentiality apply. If the engagement letter provides the member with the authority to notify HMRC in such circumstances, they should inform HMRC that they have information indicating that the accounts or statements cannot be relied upon.

7.36 If the member does not have their client's consent to the disclosure, they should write to the client and explicitly ask for permission to withdraw the report. If the client does not give consent, the member should then obtain specialist legal advice as to what action they should take.

7.37 A member should not explain to HMRC the reasons why the returns, accounts, etc. are defective. To do so without the client's consent is more likely than not to be considered by a court of law as a misuse of confidential information and an unjustified breach of client confidentiality.

Reporting to MLRO/NCA

7.38 In deciding whether a report should be made to the NCA, the member (or the member's MLRO) should take into account the various requirements of the legislation and any reporting exemption which might apply.

Professional enquiry (also known as professional clearance)

7.39 Having ceased to act, the member may be approached by a prospective adviser for information relevant to the decision of whether to accept the appointment or not.

7.40 Before a member responds to a request for information from a prospective adviser, a member must ensure that they have authority from the former client. The information to be provided should include everything that has been reasonably requested by the prospective adviser to enable them to decide whether to accept the work. The member should only discuss these matters freely with the prospective adviser if the client has given authority for them to do so.

7.41 If the client refuses permission for the member to discuss all or part of their affairs, the member should inform the prospective adviser of this fact. It is then up to the prospective adviser to make enquiries from the client as to the reasons for such a refusal.

Self-assessment

7.42 Where the error relates to a self-assessment return the client should amend any self-assessment affected by the error if they are within the time limit to do so. Where the time limit for amending a self-assessment has passed the client should provide HMRC with sufficient and accurate information to explain the error.

7.43 If HMRC fails, or is unable, to take any necessary action, for example to issue a discovery assessment, a member is under no legal obligation to draw HMRC's failure to their attention, nor to take any further action. Where it is relevant a member should ensure that the client is aware of the potential for interest and/or penalties.

Decisions of Tribunals or Courts

7.44 It is possible that after a client has made a self-assessment return a later (perhaps years later) unrelated decision of the Tribunal or Court may cast doubt on whether the self-assessment return was made on the correct basis.

7.45 A member is not under a duty to monitor all returns and all tax cases for many years after the returns have been filed to identify this rare event. However, if the member is aware of such a situation, they should determine whether the interpretation in the court or tribunal case is applicable to the client's return. The member may wish to consider seeking specialist advice if in doubt. The member should also ascertain whether the case is to be appealed and may await the outcome of any appeal. Where there is a final decision which is applicable to the client's return(s), the member should refer to the guidance below to determine what action may be required.

What corrective action is required?

7.46 If a later court or tribunal decision casts doubt on a past tax return, the action needed is a complex matter and one that presents practical difficulties.

7.47 Where the client's return is under enquiry, it remains open and can be amended in the normal manner.

7.48 The following broad principles should be applied where the client's return is not under enquiry:

7.49 Subject to whether there is any further appeal, a decision of a Court is regarded as determining how the law should always be applied. A member will however need to have regard to whether the facts of the relevant case can be distinguished from the client's circumstances.

7.50 The client should notify HMRC of the possible deficiency in their return unless:

- the basis upon which the self-assessment was made was sufficiently clear in the original return, or
- there is continuity of treatment of the item from previous returns, or
- the item was treated in accordance with prevailing practice.

7.51 The member should consider HMRC's powers to make a discovery assessment where the tax is out of normal time for assessment (generally four years).

7.52 In cases involving marketed tax avoidance schemes HMRC may assert that longer time limits apply for example where there was no disclosure at all or a DOTAS SRN was not put on the return. Members should be careful not to accept an allegation by HMRC of negligent/ careless or fraudulent/ deliberate conduct by the client or the member without seeking specialist advice first.

7.53 If a client refuses to authorise disclosure to HMRC the member should treat this situation in the same way as any other error. Unless the member has expert knowledge in this area, they should consult a specialist.

While every care has been taken in the preparation of this guidance the PCRT Bodies do not undertake a duty of care or otherwise for any loss or damage occasioned by reliance on this guidance. Practical guidance cannot and should not be taken to substitute appropriate legal advice.

8 PCRT Help sheet D: Requests for data by HMRC

Introduction

This help sheet provides guidance on the application of the ***PCRT Fundamental Principles and Standards for Tax Planning*** *in relation to requests for access to data by HMRC, including informal requests addressed to the client or to the member, formal requests to the client or to the member, Sch 36 FA 2008 statutory notices, and privileged data.*

Guidance detail

8.1 For the purposes of this help sheet the term 'data' includes documents in whatever form (including electronic) and other information. While this guidance relates to HMRC requests, other government bodies or organisations may also approach the member for data. The same principles apply.

8.2 A distinction should be drawn between a request for data made informally ('informal requests') and those requests for data which are made in exercise of a power to require the provision of the data requested ('formal requests').

8.3 Similarly, requests addressed to a client and those addressed to a member require different handling.

8.4 Where a member no longer acts for a client, the member remains subject to the duty of confidentiality. In relation to informal requests, the member should refer the enquirer either to the former client or if authorised by the client to the new agent. In relation to formal requests addressed to the member, the termination of their professional relationship with the client does not affect the member's duty to comply with that request, where legally required to do so.

8.5 A member should comply with formal requests and should not seek to frustrate legitimate requests for information. Adopting a constructive approach may help to resolve issues promptly and minimise costs to all parties.

8.6 Whilst a member should be aware of HMRC's powers it may be appropriate to take specialist advice.

8.7 Devolved tax authorities have separate powers.

8.8 Two flowcharts are at the end of this help sheet;

- Requests for data addressed to the member, and
- Requests for data addressed to the client.

Informal requests addressed to the client

8.9 From time to time HMRC chooses to communicate directly with clients rather than with the appointed agent.

8.10 HMRC has given reassurances that it is working to ensure that initial contact on compliance checks will normally be via the agent and only if the agent does not reply within an appropriate timescale will the contact be directly with the client.

8.11 When the member assists a client in dealing with such requests from HMRC, the member should advise the client that cooperation with informal requests can provide greater opportunities for the taxpayer to find a pragmatic way to work through the issue at hand with HMRC.

Informal requests addressed to the member

8.12 Disclosure in response to informal requests can only be made with the client's permission.

8.13 In many instances, the client will have authorised routine disclosure of relevant data, for example, through the engagement letter. However, if there is any doubt about whether the client has authorised disclosure, the member should ask the client to approve what is to be disclosed.

8.14 Where an oral enquiry is made by HMRC, a member should consider asking for it to be put in writing so that a response may be agreed with the client.

8.15 Although there is no obligation to comply with an informal request in whole or in part, a member should advise the client whether it is in the client's best interests to disclose such data, as lack of cooperation may have a direct impact on penalty negotiations post–enquiry.

8.16 Informal requests may be forerunners to formal requests compelling the disclosure of data. Consequently, it may be sensible to comply with such requests.

Formal requests addressed to the client

8.17 In advising their client a member should consider whether specialist advice may be needed, for example on such issues as whether the notice has been issued in accordance with the relevant tax legislation and whether the data request is valid.

8.18 The member should also advise the client about any relevant right of appeal against the formal request if appropriate and of the consequences of a failure to comply.

8.19 If the notice is legally effective the client is legally obliged to comply with the request.

8.20 The most common statutory notice issued to clients and third parties by HMRC is under Schedule 36 FA 2008 and the suggested actions are described below.

Formal requests addressed to the member

8.21 The same principles apply to formal requests to the member as formal requests to clients.

8.22 If a formal request is valid it **overrides the member's duty of confidentiality** to their client. The member is therefore obliged to comply with the request. Failure to comply with their legal obligations can expose the member to civil or criminal penalties.

8.23 In cases where the member is not legally precluded by the terms of the notice from communicating with the client, the member should advise the client of the notice and keep the client informed of progress and developments.

8.24 The member should ensure that in complying with any notice they do not provide information or data outside the scope of the notice.

8.25 If a member is faced with a situation in which HMRC is seeking to enforce disclosure by the removal of data, or seeking entrance to inspect business premises occupied by a member in their capacity as an adviser, the member should consider seeking immediate professional advice, to ensure that this is the legally correct course of action.

Schedule 36 Finance Act 2008 statutory notices

8.26 The most common statutory notice issued to clients and third parties by HMRC is under Schedule 36 FA 2008. The following notes relate only to civil enquiries; in any situation where the member knows or suspects that HMRC is undertaking a criminal investigation, specialist assistance should be sought.

8.27 Schedule 36 FA 2008 allows HMRC to require a taxpayer and/or a third party to provide data reasonably required to check the taxpayer's tax position within a specified time. HMRC can also inspect business premises and remove and/or copy data.

8.28 A member should be familiar with the rules relating to HMRC's powers to issue a Schedule 36 notice and the relevant rights of appeal and should advise only where experienced to do so. Where appropriate, experienced tax investigation assistance should be obtained.

8.29 The provisions of Schedule 36 are themselves complex and outside the scope of this guidance. The following points in relation to a member's conduct should be noted:

- HMRC can only issue a notice to a third party where it is approved by the First-Tier Tribunal or where the taxpayer to whom the notice relates agrees.
- HMRC may agree to extend any deadline for submission of the data depending on the circumstances. Any request for more time should be made well in advance of the deadline where possible.
- Schedule 36 does not allow HMRC to force entry to premises and the client can refuse HMRC entry, however this should be done only where the client has good reasons. In any such case the member should recommend that the client seeks specialist advice.

- A Schedule 36 notice does not override legal professional privilege. A member needs to be aware of this and take specialist advice where appropriate in such cases.

Privileged data

8.30 Legal privilege arises under common law and may only be overridden if this is set out in legislation. It protects a party's right to communicate in confidence with a legal adviser. The privilege belongs to the client and not to the member.

8.31 If a document is privileged: The client cannot be required to make disclosure of that document to HMRC. Another party cannot disclose it (including the member), without the client's express permission.

8.32 There are two types of legal privilege under common law: legal advice privilege and litigation privilege.

(a) **Legal advice privilege**

Covers documents passing between a client and their legal adviser prepared for the purposes of obtaining or giving legal advice. However, communications from a tax adviser who is not a practising lawyer will not attract legal advice privilege even if such individuals are giving advice on legal matters such as tax law.

(b) **Litigation privilege**

Covers data created for the dominant purpose of litigation. Litigation privilege may arise where litigation has not begun, but is merely contemplated and may apply to data prepared by non-lawyer advisors (including tax advisors). There are two important limits on litigation privilege. First, it does not arise in respect of non-adversarial proceedings. Second, the documents must be produced for the 'dominant purpose' of litigation.

8.33 A privilege under Schedule 36 paragraphs 19, (documents relating to the conduct of a pending appeal), 24 and 25 (auditors, and tax advisors' documents) might exist by "quasi-privilege" and if this is the case a tax adviser does not have to provide those documents. Care should be taken as not all data may be privileged.

8.34 A member who receives a request for data, some of which the member believes may be subject to privilege or 'quasi-privilege', should take independent legal advice on the position, unless expert in this area.

Flowchart regarding requests for data by HMRC to the Client

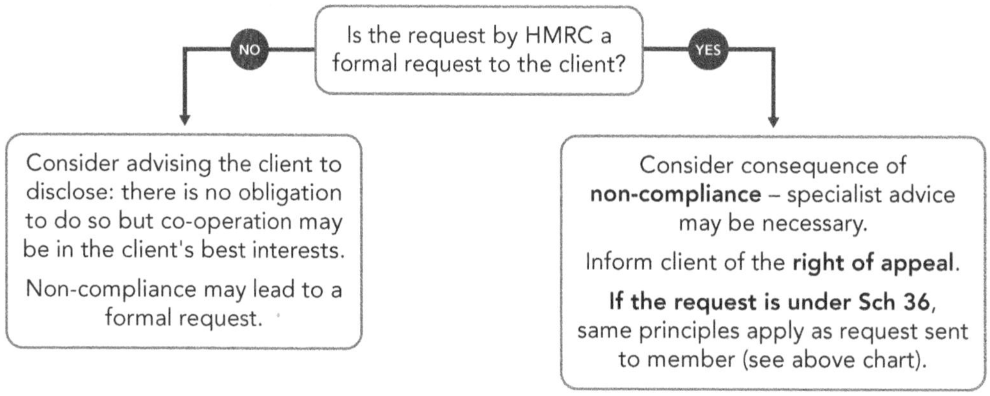

Flowchart regarding requests for data by HMRC to the Member

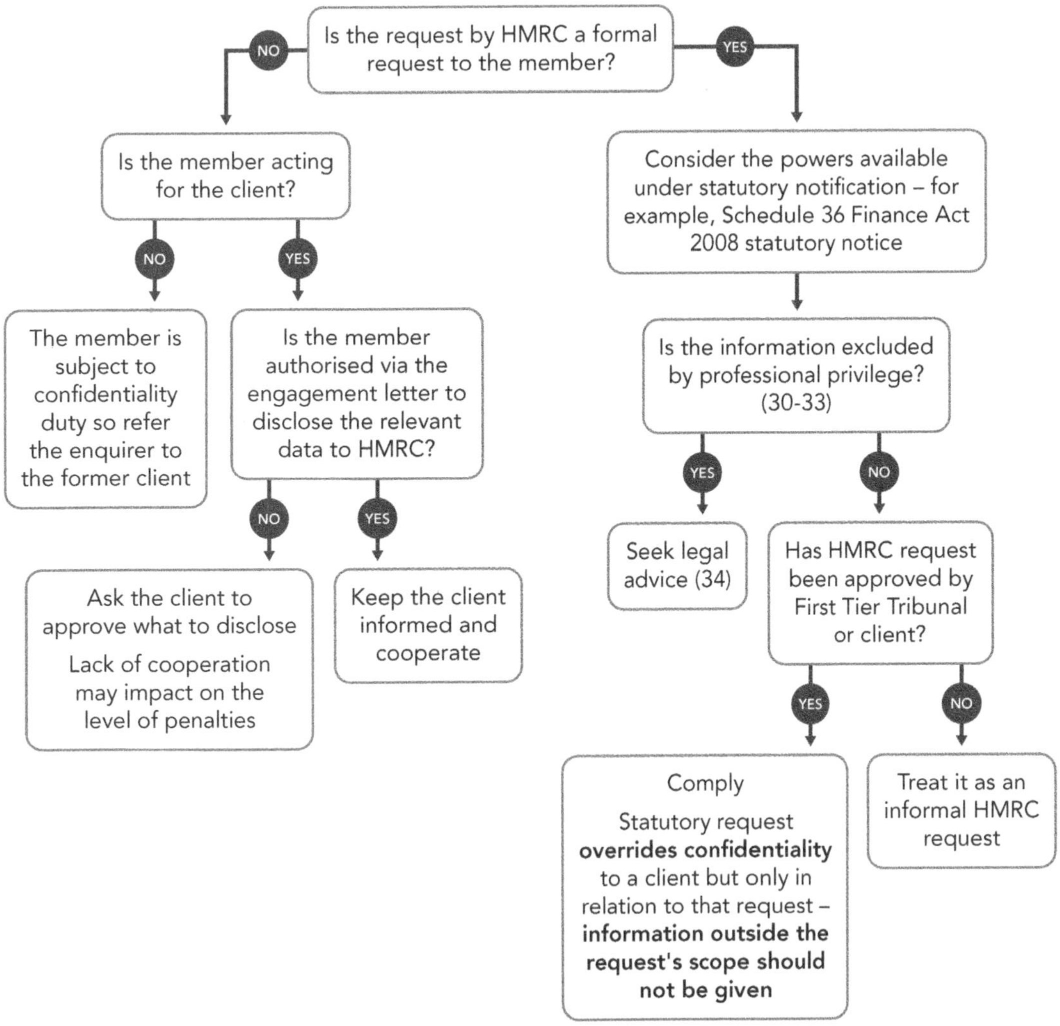

The Reference Materials have been produced by the AAT.

While every care has been taken in the preparation of this guidance the PCRT Bodies do not undertake a duty of care or otherwise for any loss or damage occasioned by reliance on this guidance. Practical guidance cannot and should not be taken to substitute appropriate legal advice.

9 PCRT Help sheet E: Members' Personal Tax Affairs

Introduction

This help sheet provides guidance on the application of the PCRT Fundamental Principles and Standards for Tax Planning in relation to a members' personal tax affairs and covers the following areas:

- *Tax returns and tax compliance*
- *Disputes with HMRC and advocacy*
- *Tax planning*

Application

9.1 The content of this guidance is primarily applicable to members in professional practice but the principles apply to all members dealing with their own tax affairs and those of any other person or those with whom the member has a personal relationship, for example, family members and friends.

9.2 A member should always act in a way that will not bring the member or their professional body into disrepute.

Tax returns and tax compliance

9.3 A member's own tax affairs should be kept up to date. Neglect of a member's own affairs could raise doubts within HMRC as to the standard of the member's professional work and could bring the member or their professional body into disrepute.

Disputes with HMRC and advocacy

9.4 A member who is in dispute with HMRC regarding their own tax affairs may wish to consider engaging an agent to represent them.

Tax planning

9.5 A member should consider whether any tax arrangements with which they might be associated on their own behalf might bring the member and the profession into disrepute. In this regard, members are referred to the guidance set out in **Help sheet B: Tax Advice**.

While every care has been taken in the preparation of this guidance the PCRT Bodies do not undertake a duty of care or otherwise for any loss or damage occasioned by reliance on this guidance. Practical guidance cannot and should not be taken to substitute appropriate legal advice.

Tax tables 2025/26

This document may be changed to reflect periodical updates in the computer-based assessment, so please check you have the most recent version while studying. (Tax tables are up to date as at 25/07/2025.)

1 Tax rates and bands

Tax rates	Tax bands	Normal rates %	Dividend rates %
Basic rate	£1–£37,700	20	8.75
Higher rate	£37,701–£125,140	40	33.75
Additional rate	£125,141 and over	45	39.35

2 Allowances

		£
Personal allowance		12,570
Savings allowance:	Basic rate taxpayer	1,000
	Higher rate taxpayer	500
Dividend allowance		500
Income limit for personal allowances*		100,000

* Personal allowances are reduced by £1 for every £2 over the income limit.

3 Property income allowance

	£
Annual limit	1,000

4 Individual savings accounts

	£
Annual limit	20,000

5 Residence

Residence	Criteria
Automatically not resident	Must have been UK resident in 1 or more of the 3 tax years immediately preceding the relevant tax year and have spent fewer than 16 days in the UK: or
	Must not have been UK resident in any of the 3 tax years immediately preceding the relevant tax year and have spent fewer than 46 days in the UK: or
	Works full time overseas, spends less than 91 days in the UK, has no significant breaks in overseas working and works less than 31 days in the UK.

Residence	Criteria
Automatically resident	Spent 183 or more days in the UK in the tax year; or
	Only home is in the UK and owned, rented or lived in the home for at least 91 days and spent at least 30 days there in the tax year; or
	75% of total working days in a 365-day period is in the UK.
Resident by number of ties	If UK resident for one or more of the previous three tax years: • 4 ties needed if spend 16–45 days in the UK • 3 ties needed if spend 46–90 days in the UK • 2 ties needed if spend 91–120 days in the UK • 1 tie needed if spend over 120 days in the UK
	If UK resident in none of the previous three tax years • 4 ties needed if spend 46–90 days in the UK • 3 ties needed if spend 91–120 days in the UK • 2 ties needed if spend over 120 days in the UK

6 Car benefit percentage

CO2 Emissions for petrol engines g/km	Electric range miles	%
Nil		3
1 to 50	130 or more	3
1 to 50	70-129	6
1 to 50	40-69	9
1 to 50	30-39	13
1 to 50	Less than 30	15
51 to 54		16
55 or more		17 + 1% for every extra 5g/km above 55g/km

7 Car fuel benefit

	£
Base figure	28,200

8 Approved mileage allowance payments (employees and residential landlords)

First 10,000 miles	45p per mile
Over 10,000 miles	25p per mile
Additional passengers	5p per mile per passenger

Motorcycles	24p per mile
Bicycles	20p per mile

9 Van benefit charge

	£
Basic charge	4,020
Private fuel charge	769
Benefit charge for zero emission vans	NIL

10 Other benefits in kind

Expensive accommodation limit	£75,000
Health screening	One per year
Incidental overnight expenses: within UK	£5 per night
Incidental overnight expenses: overseas	£10 per night
Job-related accommodation	£Nil
Living expenses where job-related exemption applies	Restricted to 10% of employees net earnings
Loan of assets annual charge	20%
Low-rate or interest free loans	Up to £10,000
Mobile telephones	One per employee
Non-cash gifts from someone other than the employer	£250 per tax year
Non-cash long service award	£50 per year of service
Pay whilst attending a full-time course	£15,480 per academic year
Provision of eye tests and spectacles for DSE (display screen equipment)	£Nil
Provision of parking spaces	£Nil
Provision of workplace childcare	£Nil
Provision of workplace sports facilities	£Nil
Removal and relocation expenses	£8,000
Staff party or event	£150 per head
Staff suggestion scheme	Up to £5,000
Subsidised meals	£Nil
Working from home	£6 per week / £26 per month

11 HMRC official rate

	%
HMRC official rate	3.75

12 National insurance contributions

		%
Class 1 Employee:	Below £12,570	0
	Above £12,570 and Below £50,270	8
	£50,270 and above	2
Class 1 Employer:	Below £5,000	0
	£5,000 and above	15
Class 1A		15
		£
Employment allowance		10,500

13 Capital gains tax

		£
Annual exempt amount		3,000

14 Capital gains tax - tax rates

		%
Basic rate		18
Higher rate		24

15 Inheritance tax – tax rates

		£
Nil rate band		325,000
Additional residence nil-rate band*		175,000
		%
Excess taxable at:	Death rate	40
	Lifetime rate	20

*Applies when a home is passed on death to direct descendants of the deceased after 6 April 2017. Any unused band is transferrable to a spouse or civil partner.

16 Inheritance tax – tapering relief

		% reduction
3 years or less		0
Over 3 years but less than 4 years		20
Over 4 years but less than 5 years		40
Over 5 years but less than 6 years		60
Over 6 years but less than 7 years		80

17 Inheritance – exemptions

		£
Small gifts	250 per transferee per tax year	
Marriage or civil partnership:	From parent	5,000
	Grandparent	2,500
	One party to the other	2,500
	Others	1,000
Annual exemption		3,000

Tell us what you think

Got comments or feedback on this book? Let us know.
Use your QR code reader:

Or, visit:
https://www.smartsurvey.co.uk/s/GPUBYI/

Need to get in touch with customer service?

www.bpp.com/request-support

Spotted an error?

https://learningmedia.bpp.com/pages/errata

TP02-1-23026-0004